Welcome to
Being Vegan

There are many reasons why people decide to go vegan. We typically associate this lifestyle with the issue of animal welfare, or the pursuit of a healthier diet. More recently, however, veganism has gained huge popularity among those with environmental concerns, too.

Changing our diets is one of the most significant things that we as individuals can do to reduce our impact on the planet. With more and more people choosing to go vegan, it's never been easier to make the change to ethical and plant-based living.

Being Vegan is the ultimate guide for anyone who is embracing this way of life, whether you are a newbie or a veteran vegan, or perhaps just a curious flexitarian. This special edition is packed with over 30 delicious recipes for every occasion, including a show-stopping dinner party menu sure to impress even the most staunch non-vegans. You'll also find a selection of features that we hope you'll find useful on your vegan journey, covering health, beauty, fashion, lifestyle, sustainability and more.

sona
BOOKS

First published in the UK 2021 by Sona Books
an imprint of Danann Media Publishing Ltd.

Editor for Danann Tom O'Neill

Images courtesy of:
Getty Images; Ananas Anam; Shutterstock / gowithstock;
Chesterfields of England; @amymaysews

CAT NO: **SON0474**
ISBN: **978-1-912918-26-3**

Made in EU.

For Juliette O'Neill. Enjoy!!

Contents

Introduction **10**
Beate Sonerud

Vegan Myths Busted **12**
Rebecca Greig

Food & Recipes

Top Tips, Tricks & Hacks **20**
Rebecca Greig

Vegan Substitutes **22**
Rebecca Greig

Make Your Own Dairy Alternatives ... **26**
Rebecca Greig

Eating with the Seasons **28**
Victoria Williams

Recipe Index

Light Bites

Granola Bars **32**
Buddha Bowls **34**
Tabbouleh with Hummus and Pita ... **36**
Momos & Chutney **38**
Soy Nuggets & Sweet Potato Fries **40**
Ratatouille & Seeded Loaf **42**
Green Bean and Grilled Tofu Salad .. **44**
Stuffed Squash **46**
Spring Rolls with Dipping Sauce **48**
Pumpkin Soup **50**
Breaded Tofu Bites & Satay Sauce..... **52**
Grilled Veg Feast **54**

Main Meals

Vegetable Soup **56**
Courgetti Bolognese **58**
Sweet Potato and Chickpea Curry **60**
Yaki Soba **62**
Red Thai Curry **64**
Ultimate Burger **66**
Cauliflower and Bean Chilli **68**

Sweet Treats

Oatmeal Cookies **70**
Raw Blueberry Cheesecake **72**
Energy Balls **74**
Matcha Cake **76**

Coconut Macaroons **78**

Raw Chocolate Brownies **80**

Blueberry & Almond Cake **82**

Chocolate Celebration Cake **84**

Pumpkin Spice Loaf **86**

Vanilla Cake **88**

Fudge **90**

Peanut Brownies **92**

Dinner Party Menu

Purple Sushi **95**

Rainbow Veg Lasagne **96**

Raw Pistachio & Carrot Cake **97**

Lifestyle & Sustainability

Are You Vegan Enough? **100**
Rebecca Greig

Being Vegan on a Budget **106**
Victoria Williams

The Power of Plant Protein **110**
Beate Sonerud

The Vegan Home **112**
Joanne Al-Samarae

Health & Beauty **114**
Alice Barnes-Brown

Fashion with a Conscience **118**
Joanne Al-Samarae

Fighting the Throwaway Culture **120**
Victoria Williams

Eco-Friendly Travel **126**
Joanne Al-Samarae

How to be a Globetrotting Vegan **130**
Alice Barnes-Brown

Welcome to Veganism

Veganism is on the rise, driven by environmental and health concerns, as well as the protection of animal welfare

Waitrose found that 5% of people between 18 and 34 are now dietary vegans, while for those older than 55, the share dips down to a tiny 1%.

Y ou may have picked up this book because you're a veteran vegan, a recent convert or just curious about changing your diet and lifestyle. Veganism is now more popular than ever, but what does it mean to 'be vegan'? And what's behind this seismic shift in our attitudes?

Vegan goes mainstream

2019 is the year of the vegan, according to *The Economist*. Over the last decade, there has been an explosion in interest in veganism: on the scale from 0 to 100 that online search engine Google uses to measure interest in a search term, 'veganism' skyrocketed from 17 in 2008 to 88 in 2018.

In the UK, the total number of dietary vegans quadrupled from 2014 to 2018, according to the Vegan Society. Though as a share of the population, vegans remain a small minority: a study by supermarket chain

Why go vegan

When the term 'vegan diet' was first coined in 1944, it referred specifically to removing all animal products from your diet for ethical reasons of animal welfare. Today, anyone who fully gives up animal food products, regardless of motivation, would qualify for the vegan label. While animal welfare remains the primary motivator, it is not the only one. A survey of vegans and vegetarians found that people often had several reasons for adopting their lifestyle: as well as animal welfare (cited by 55% of participants), health benefits (45%) and environmental concerns (38%) were also deciding factors. With the rising awareness of the climate crisis, the huge environmental benefits of removing animal food products from our diets will likely see veganism gain increasing traction.

Is a plant-based diet vegan?

The term 'plant-based diet' has also gained huge popularity in recent years. At first glance, it may simply seem like a synonym for a vegan diet. But while you can most definitely be vegan and plant-based, not all vegans are plant-based, and not all those adopting a plant-based diet would classify as vegans. Sound confusing? Well, those on a plant-based diet eat unprocessed foods, such as fruits, vegetables and whole grains. So, processed vegan foods (such as the vegan chicken offerings trialled by KFC in collaboration with Beyond Meat) may not make the cut for those committed to a plant-based diet. Some people on a plant-based diet may also choose to eat tiny amounts of animal products; since the concept of a plant-based diet emerged from the health community rather than the animal welfare community, it doesn't necessarily exclude animal products completely, only on minimising their intake to optimise health.

Vegan food options are becoming far more accessible

Beyond diet: a vegan lifestyle

Veganism is most commonly associated with food, but fully adopting a vegan lifestyle requires the exclusion of all forms of animal cruelty. This means using no leather products, wool or silk, as well as avoiding products that are tested on animals, and shying away from events where animals are used for entertainment (such as circuses or horse riding). Understandably, this more extensive vegan lifestyle is less common than dietary veganism: in the UK for example, while there were an estimated 542,000 dietary vegans in 2016, there were only 360,000 lifestyle vegans.

Where next?

The rapid growth in veganism, particularly of the dietary kind, is likely to continue. With awareness of the climate crisis intensifying, more individuals will look to reduce their carbon footprints – and a vegan diet is one of the most impactful actions available. Awareness of the significant health impacts of our diets is also on the rise: poor diet now kills more people globally than smoking, according to a study released in April 2019. As more vegan options are becoming readily available, translating motivation to action is becoming easier than ever.

"In the UK, the number of dietary vegans quadrupled between 2014 and 2018"

Global veganism would dramatically decrease the amount of land needed to produce food

WHAT IF THE WORLD WENT VEGAN?

If everyone globally went vegan, we would see a whopping 49% cut in greenhouse gas emissions, a 76% reduction in land used to produce food and a 19% reduction in fresh water withdrawals, according to a 2018 study from Oxford University. Universal veganism would also help our deteriorating ecosystems and biodiversity, as it would lead to a 49% reduction in eutrophication, where fertilisers leak into lakes and rivers with harmful effects on nature and wildlife. By 2050, if everyone went vegan we could avoid 8.1 million deaths, as a reduction of red meat consumption coupled with increased fruit and vegetable intake and a reduction in calories would lead to a significant drop in obesity levels, according to a 2016 study (also by Oxford University). And the cherry on top: we could see healthcare-related savings and avoid climate damage racking up to $1.5 trillion by 2050.

Vegan Myths
BUSTED

Although veganism is more popular than ever, misconceptions about the lifestyle persist. Let's take a look at some vegan myths and find out why they are just that

1

"You'll miss out"

One of the biggest things that stop people going vegan is a fear of missing out. You'll miss cheese-covered pizza or nachos and your favourite chocolate bar. However, you are actually more likely to crave these junk foods when you eat them frequently, so eventually, once you have eliminated them, you'll stop craving them. Soon you'll be whipping up delicious vegan treats, and the tasty non-vegan junk food will be a distant memory.

2

"You won't be as healthy"

Many people believe that the absence of meat is a problem because you'll end up lacking nutrients that you'll only get from meat. Vegans are actually far more likely to eat the recommended daily allowance of fruit and vegetables, plus have lower rates of obesity.

3

"You will automatically be healthier"

We wish! Obviously, if you are eating a variety of fresh produce packed with vitamins, yes you might be healthier. However, you can just eat chips and crisps and still be a vegan. Unfortunately the unhealthy vegan diet can be starchy and potato based; often chips are still the only vegan option in some restaurants – although this is rapidly changing.

4

"Vegans don't eat oysters or mussels"

This is a widely debated subject in the vegan community. Some vegans do actually eat them and believe that these bivalves are acceptable for vegans. Many become vegan for environmental or ethical reasons. Research has found eating oysters and mussels is actually environmentally sustainable as well as nutritious. There's also some evidence that they don't feel pain and because they don't have a brain or heart then this deals with the ethical issue. Many do disagree, but really it is personal opinion. If your love of oysters is what is stopping you from being vegan, then carry on without the guilt!

5

"Vegans Never Get Sick"

This is a myth that has actually been spread by vegans themselves. There is no scientific proof that vegans are ill less often than those who eat meat and dairy. On either diet, if you eat well and maintain a healthy diet mixed with exercise, chances are your immune system will be stronger – but it isn't necessarily anything to do with being vegan.

6

"All Vegans Are Deficient In Calcium"

Just because vegans don't consume dairy products, this doesn't mean they will be lacking in calcium, like many believe. Although milk is high in calcium, our bodies don't actually absorb much of it, so it isn't the most efficient source anyway. As long as your vegan diet is packed with a good balance of cruciferous vegetables, like kale and cabbage, you'll be laughing. They tend to be high in calcium, and the mineral is readily bioavailable, which means our bodies are able to absorb it more efficiently.

7

"Vegans Are Weak"

It's widely assumed that strength comes from protein in meat, so a meat-free diet will make us weak, but there is no proof of this. Many athletes, including NFL defensive end David Carter and ultra marathoner Matt Frazier, are at their optimal strength on a meat-free diet. Consuming enough protein is recommended for those working out frequently to aid muscle repair. It's often thought that vegans don't get enough, but on average vegetarians and vegans eat 70% more protein than the recommended daily intake; meat eaters eat almost double.

8

"You'll Always Be Hungry"

As long as you drink enough water and eat a balance of food packed with healthy fats and fibre, it's easy to feel satisfied on a vegan diet. Going vegan might mean snacking habits change and you'll be reaching for a bag of nuts or raisins instead of a chocolate bar, but you shouldn't be hungry. If anything, your high-fibre diet will keep you feeling fuller for longer.

9

"Pregnant Women Shouldn't Be Vegan"

The importance of nutrition for pregnant women and babies in the womb should never be underestimated. It is possible to get all of the adequate nutritional levels from a whole-food and plant-based diet as long as you eat enough calories and get enough specific nutrients such as B12, iron, D3 and omega-3. If you are pregnant and vegan, talk to your doctor or a nutritionist who specialises in pre- and post-natal nutrition for the best advice.

10

"It's expensive"

Just because vegans don't consume dairy products, this doesn't mean they will be lacking in calcium, like many believe. Although milk is high in calcium, our bodies don't actually absorb much of it, so it isn't the most efficient source anyway. As long as your vegan diet is packed with a good balance of cruciferous vegetables, like kale and cabbage, you'll be laughing. They tend to be high in calcium, and the mineral is readily bioavailable, which means our bodies are able to absorb it more efficiently.

Food & Recipes

Food & Recipes

Top Tips, Tricks & Hacks **20**
Rebecca Greig

Vegan Substitutes **22**
Rebecca Greig

Make Your Own Dairy Alternatives ...**26**
Rebecca Greig

Eating with the Seasons.....................**28**
Victoria Williams

Recipe Index
Light Bites

Granola Bars **32**

Buddha Bowls **34**

Tabbouleh with Hummus and Pita ...**36**
Momos & Chutney **38**
Soy Nuggets & Sweet Potato Fries **40**
Ratatouille & Seeded Loaf **42**
Green Bean and Grilled Tofu Salad ..**44**
Stuffed Squash **46**
Spring Rolls with Dipping Sauce **48**
Pumpkin Soup **50**
Breaded Tofu Bites & Satay Sauce.....**52**
Grilled Veg Feast **54**

Main Meals

Vegetable Soup **56**
Courgetti Bolognese **58**
Sweet Potato and Chickpea Curry **60**
Yaki Soba **62**
Red Thai Curry **64**
Ultimate Burger **66**
Cauliflower and Bean Chilli **68**

Sweet Treats

Oatmeal Cookies **70**
Raw Blueberry Cheesecake **72**
Energy Balls **74**
Matcha Cake **76**
Coconut Macaroons **78**
Raw Chocolate Brownies **80**
Blueberry & Almond Cake **82**
Chocolate Celebration Cake **84**
Pumpkin Spice Loaf **86**
Vanilla Cake **88**
Fudge **90**
Peanut Brownies **92**

Dinner Party Menu

Purple Sushi **95**
Rainbow Veg Lasagne **96**
Raw Pistachio & Carrot Cake **97**

Vegan tips, tricks & hacks

Stock your cupboards with essential ingredients that will help you make the tastiest most flavourful vegan food possible

3 Embrace nutritional yeast

Nutritional yeast is used in a lot of vegan cooking. It's a food additive made from a single-celled organism, Saccharomyces cerevisiae, which is grown on molasses. Packed with B vitamins, folic acid, selenium, zinc and protein, it is also low in fat, but actually it is often used mainly for its taste. It has a distinctive cheesy or nutty taste that is great for adding depth to sauces, or it is very effective for making vegan cheese sauces. Try it sprinkled on popcorn or pasta dishes, or mixed into mashed potato.

1 Add savoury depth

There are a few must-have ingredients for adding depth to your sauces and soups. Add some tomatoes to your vegetable soup to create an almost buttery taste, or a decent splash of white wine can add a lovely savoury depth to your sauces. Keep a bottle of vegan Worcestershire sauce on hand for adding a meaty taste to your cooking – it's amazing in a bolognese sauce. Mild miso sauce is also a must-have ingredient.

Stock up on spices

Following the vegan diet may mean avoiding a whole host of ingredients, but it doesn't mean you have to lose out on flavour. Make sure you stock up your spice rack so you can cook flavourful dishes. Spices like smoked paprika, turmeric, garlic powder, ginger and nutmeg are essential, while pre-mixed spices like Cajun, Italian seasoning and garam masala can liven up a range of meals.

4 Download VeGuide

VeGuide is a handy app made by The Vegan Society to help users embark on the vegan journey. It provides first-time vegans with step-by-step guides on cutting out animal products, as well as daily videos guiding you into the vegan lifestyle. The app includes a daily quiz that, once completed, will provide you with new recipes and vegan discounts. The recipes can be stored in your recipe bank for future use.

5 Always keep olive oil to hand

A simple splash of olive oil can really enhance the flavours in a dish. Drizzle some over your homemade hummus, pasta or even on some cakes.

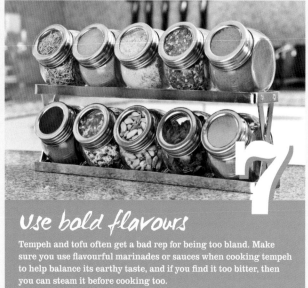

7 Use bold flavours

Tempeh and tofu often get a bad rep for being too bland. Make sure you use flavourful marinades or sauces when cooking tempeh to help balance its earthy taste, and if you find it too bitter, then you can steam it before cooking too.

6

Press tofu

To improve the texture of your tofu, press it – it will make it firmer, more palatable, and remove the excess water. Use a special tofu press, or sandwich it between two chopping boards with a weight on top to squish it down. Leave it for a minimum of 30 minutes, but a couple of hours is better.

8 Beans for all

Beans are packed with fibre and a great source of protein – always keep dried and canned beans in your cupboard. They are very versatile and can be used in salads, curries, stews, soups burgers and even sweet treats like brownies!

10 A squeeze of citrus

Squeeze some fresh lime juice over your salad, along with some chilli flakes or lemon juice and a pinch of black pepper, for a tasty and super-low calorie dressing. It will also give you a boost of vitamin C. Fresh lime juice drizzled over a soy-sauce-based stir-fry works as a great taste enhancer, and let's not forget that any spare limes can be used to make a refreshing mojito or daiquiri.

9 Use aquafaba

Use the liquid in your can of chickpeas as an awesome egg replacement in your baking. Use an electric whisk to make it light and fluffy, and fold it in to your favourite cake mixes. It is also great for binding ingredients together for when you are making veggie burgers or bhajis.

Vegan Substitutes

Don't miss out on your favourite foods when you go vegan

Vegan cooking has never been easier, with so many alternative ingredients that you can swap out of non-vegan recipes. From ingenious egg replacement hacks to different fats that can be swapped in for butter, you'll never struggle to find something that will work for you. There are many meat alternatives on offer, too, meaning you can still get plenty of important protein and nutrients, and you won't be lacking in iron or key B vitamins – as is commonly (yet wrongly) assumed. Just about every coffee shop now offers great dairy-free milk options to suit your tastes, and you won't have to miss out on comfort foods, such as pizza and mac and cheese, with the various vegan cheese alternatives out there.

Seitan

Seitan is made from wheat gluten and contains a comparable amount of protein to red meat. It is also a very good source of iron and phosphorous. To make seitan taste like actual meat, you should season it in the same way as you would season meat.

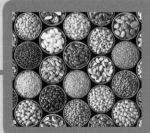

Legumes

Although they don't taste like meat, legumes like black beans, pinto beans and lentils have similar nutrients to red meat. They are also a very good source of protein for vegans, are rich in carbohydrates and healthy fibre, as well as being high in iron, zinc and phosphorous like red meat.

Tempeh

Made from fermented soya beans, tempeh is a protein-rich meat substitute. Like red meat, tempeh will provide vegans with iron, zinc, phosphorous and B vitamins. Tempeh can be used in stir fries instead of steak or sliced in sandwiches.

Red meat (beef, lamb)

Red meat is a source of protein, which helps to keep muscles and bones strong, as well as iron, zinc and other antioxidants to keep your immune system functioning. It also contains vitamin B12, which is needed for DNA and keeps our blood cells and nerves healthy. However, it is one of the worst foods for its environmental impact, and consumption of too much red meat has been linked to cancer, heart disease and other serious health risks.

Tofu

Tofu is a great source of protein and it contains all of the nine essential amino acids. Although it doesn't contain all of the same nutrients as poultry, tofu is a good source of iron, calcium, manganese, selenium, copper, zinc, magnesium and phosphorous.

TVP

Textured Vegetable Protein is an easy-to-use and cheap meat replacement, and can be adapted into many different dishes to replace both red and white meat. It is made from dehydrated soy and comes in granules that you have to rehydrate. It is a good source of protein as well as iron.

Cauliflower

While not particularly similar, cauliflower works really well sliced and fried like a chicken steak or coated in a batter for chicken-style fried cauliflower to satisfy your fried chicken craving. Cauliflower is low-calorie and contains 11% of your recommended daily intake of vitamin B6.

White meat (poultry)

Similar to red meat, white meat is very nutritious. It is a great source of protein, niacin, phosphorous, vitamins B6 and B12, calcium, iron and zinc. 100g of chicken breast contains one-third of your daily intake of vitamin B6 and 86% of niacin. Chicken, however, is one of the most consumed meats around the world, so millions of poultry birds are slaughtered per year.

Pork

Pork is high in protein and contains many nutrients that promote a healthy body. Much like chicken, it contains all nine of the essential amino acids, which are vital for your body's repair, plus iron, phosphorous, B12, B6, selenium, niacin and zinc.

Jackfruit

Jackfruit is versatile and can be slow cooked in much the same way as pulled pork, and has a very similar texture. It doesn't contain much protein in comparison to the actual meats but it does have essential nutrients like magnesium and copper.

Aquafaba

Aquafaba is the water in which chickpeas have been cooked, and is often used to replace egg whites in cooking. When legumes are cooked their carbohydrates and proteins migrate into the cooking water and creates a liquid that is able to act very similarly to egg whites.

Ground flax

Combine one tablespoon of ground flax (also called flaxseed or linseed) with three tablespoons of water and leave for a few minutes. The mix becomes thick and gelatinous, sort of like an egg. Use this to replace each egg in your recipe.

Applesauce

Applesauce is a really great egg substitute because it helps to bind everything together, adds moisture and is pretty low in fat. Simply use a third of a cup to replace each egg in your recipe and your cakes or cookies should turn our perfectly – and not tasting of apple.

Eggs

Eggs are used in so much of our everyday cooking, whether you eat them on their own or baked into a dish. They are used to set and bind foods, as well as being a great source of protein. One egg has 7g of quality protein as well as iron, vitamins and minerals. Concerns around battery farming and the killing of male chicks means vegans abstain from eggs.

Honey

Honey contains many nutrients and vitamins and is rich in antioxidants. Honey is also a healthier sweetener than proper sugar. Honey is known to lower cholesterol and manage blood pressure. Growing concerns about the bee population and their exploitation, however, have led people to question and cut down on their consumption of this important natural product.

Maple syrup

Maple syrup is actually healthier than honey and can be used in baking to replace refined sugar. It contains antioxidants, calcium and has a surprising number of health benefits, including improving skin, digestion and inflammation.

Golden syrup

Golden syrup is nowhere near as healthy as maple syrup, but it is delightfully sweet and sticky – much like honey. Flavour your dairy-free porridge with it or drizzle it on top of your vegan pancakes – but do so in moderation!

Butter

Butter has a very high fat content and can be used in a variety of recipes and as a key ingredient in many cakes and other baked goods. It is rich in flavour and is used as a spread to add flavour to bread, crackers and more.

Cheese

Cheese is full of protein, fat and various vitamins and nutrients like calcium, zinc, B2, B12, magnesium and phosphorous. It can be used to flavour various dishes almost like a seasoning and to bind ingredients when cooking. However, it is very high in fat.

Soy milk

Soy milk is generally a bit thicker than other plant-based milks and has more protein, but has less calcium and nutrients. It does have a tendency to curdle when making coffee and other hot drinks, so you may have to change how you prepare your drinks slightly.

Almond milk

Almond milk can taste a little watery when you make the switch, and doesn't have as much protein as cow's milk. However, one cup of almond milk has 56% of your daily intake of calcium.

Oat milk

Oat milk is the creamiest of the other substitutes and is a very tasty, nutrient-rich milk substitute. It contains more than ten times the calcium than soy milk and has more protein than almond milk. It is also really good for making creamy barista-style coffees.

Vegan margarine

This is a great butter substitute, but it can make cakes a little oily and, depending on the brand, may taint the taste of buttercream if you are baking. On the plus side, it is softer that real butter and lower in calories, which can benefit your baking.

Oils

There are loads of delicious cake recipes that use oil instead of butter. Cakes made with oil are often lighter in texture and more moist. You can often use sunflower oil, olive oil, groundnut oil, coconut oil, vegetable oil, avocado oil and more.

Nutritional yeast flakes

Nutritional yeast is deactivated yeast and is either a yellow powder or in the form of yellow flakes. It has a slightly cheesy flavour, so it is often used in recipes to make dairy-free cheese sauces for things like macaroni and cauliflower cheese.

Vegan cheese

This often comes in slices or is grated and can be used on the top of pizza or in toasties and sandwiches. It doesn't melt in the same way as real cheese, but it's a pretty close replacement to the real thing – and vegan cheeses are getting better by the minute.

Milk

Cow's milk contains many nutrients. It is full of calcium, which is pretty much essential for your bones and blood pressure. However, it is controversial because of the high amount of hormones and fat it has within it, as well as ethical concerns surrounding the dairy industry.

Make Your Own Cheese and Milk

Don't just rely on the shops for your dairy alternatives when it's so simple to create them at home

Although non-dairy vegan products are becoming more accessible in supermarkets, they can be more expensive than the dairy equivalents. Making your own is often far cheaper, plus it is actually easier than you'd think. The great thing about making cheese and milk yourself means that you'll know exactly what is in them and they'll taste fresher too.

Vegan 'Mozzarella' Balls

 12 SERVINGS

 **10-15 mins PREP TIME**

 4-8 hrs REST TIME

INGREDIENTS

- 500 ml | 17½ fl oz | 2⅛ cups unsweetened soya yogurt
- 1 tsp salt
- 200 ml | 7 fl oz | ⅞ cups extra virgin olive oil

RECIPE

1 Place a cheese/muslin cloth in a sieve over a large mixing bowl, then add the salt to the yogurt before tipping it into the muslin.

2 Wrap the cloth tightly around the yogurt and secure it with twine. Now attach a hook to the bag so that it hangs over the bowl for 24 hours.

3 Drain the liquid from the bowl and place the muslin over the sieve. Use a heavy plate or heavy chopping board to weigh it down for a further 24 hours.

4 Tip the yogurt into a clean bowl and stir it vigorously until it is smooth.

5 Sterilise a jar to store the mozzarella in. Next, coat your hands in olive oil and carefully roll the yogurt into 12 cheese balls. Pop them in the jar with the extra virgin olive oil and store for up to 3 weeks in a cool, dry place. Once opened, keep in the fridge and use within a few days.

Vegan cheese is a growing industry, but some types are simple to make at home

Add garlic cloves, olives or dried herbs to the jar for extra flavour

Homemade Oat Milk

SERVINGS

5 mins
PREP TIME

INGREDIENTS

- 950 ml | 33½ fl oz | 4 cups water
- 90 g | 3 oz | 1 cup rolled oats

RECIPE

1 Place the rolled oats and water in a blender on high speed for 30-45 seconds.

2 Strain the milk through a clean t-shirt or tea towel – strain twice for the best results.

3 Store the milk in the fridge and enjoy on its own, with coffee or in your cereal. Shake well before each use!

Don't blend the mixture for more than 45 seconds, as it will become slimy

Replace the oats with nuts (soaked overnight, drained and rinsed) to create nut milk

Eating
with the
Seasons

**From flavour to finances, there
are many benefits to eating
locally and seasonally**

Thanks to modern agriculture, new processing methods and quick transport, we're used to being able to go to the shops and find our favourite fruits, vegetables, fungi and exotic foods in stock year-round. It's normal now to see strawberries on the shelves in December, and there's nothing unusual about finding oranges from South Africa and bananas from Colombia. This is a very recent convenience; for most of human history, people survived by working with the seasons and eating the food that grew well in their region. As nice as it is to have whatever you want, whenever you want it, there are arguments for returning to this more natural way of eating.

You've probably noticed that the price of fresh produce fluctuates, with some costing twice as much in winter. It's simple supply and demand – when fruits and vegetables are abundant and can be grown locally with less effort, they can be sold at a lower price. When farmers have to grow produce in heated tunnels or greenhouses and work harder for a smaller crop, or when food has to be imported from other countries, prices go up to cover the extra costs, and consumers fork out to satisfy their cravings. Other factors like crop failures and bad weather affect the price and availability of both local and imported produce, but the season is one of the most consistent drivers of cost.

Recent surveys have found that we're increasingly disconnected from our food. Few people know the natural growing seasons of fruits and vegetables, and a quarter of British children are unaware that carrots grow underground. Shopping at farm shops and local markets means customers can meet the producers and ask them questions about how the food was grown and how best to cook it. Perhaps someone else browsing the stall will overhear and share a tip or a recipe. These interactions help keep the local community alive and ensure knowledge about your food and your local area is not lost.

Although food miles are a surprisingly small percentage of the overall environmental impact of food production, they still add up. Food flown or shipped in from abroad often has to be refrigerated or stored in wax, and the whole process requires more packaging to make sure produce is still fresh and unblemished by the time it reaches the shops. By buying locally, you minimise the distance your food has travelled from farm to plate, you can take it home in a paper bag or your own containers, and it's easier to find out about the conditions it was grown and processed in.

Food grown for supermarkets must meet strict cosmetic standards; lemons have to be smooth and bright, apples perfectly round, and strawberries over a certain size. Millions of tons of food are wasted every year in the UK alone, and this is partly due to our rejection of anything less than perfect. Since 2009, shops have been allowed to sell 'wonky' fruit and veg, but it's only begun to catch on recently. At a farm shop or market you'll find straight carrots alongside wonky ones, and remembering that they all taste the same once they're chopped up and cooked can help to reduce the amount of food households and producers throw away.

Local, in-season fruits and vegetables are picked once they've ripened perfectly on the plant, giving them maximum flavour. When produce is grown

> "surveys have found we're increasingly disconnected from our food"

abroad or out of season, it often has to be picked early and chilled for transportation so it's not over-ripe or spoiled when it goes on the shelves. Some foods, like bananas, continue to ripen once they've been removed from the plant, but others have to be artificially heated and ripened when they arrive at their destination. This chilling and heating can affect the flavour and texture, leading to watery fruits and limp greens. Nutrient levels can also begin to drop if food is stored for a long time or processed incorrectly; while many producers now have methods that keep their fruits and vegetables as fresh and nutritious as possible, buying whole produce locally is the best way to guarantee you're eating food at its best. If there are fruits and vegetables you really can't go without in the months they're out of season, consider buying them while they're in season and preserving them – lots of produce freezes or dries well, and foods that won't survive the freezer can make excellent jams, pickles and chutneys.

If you've grown bored of cooking or you tend to stick to the same foods throughout the year, challenging yourself to eat more local and seasonal food might be the shake-up you need. Not only will eating produce when it's in season increase variety in your diet, it will also push you to be more creative in the kitchen. Seasonal foods lend

Many of us have lost touch with our food and its production

Head to a market and you can buy fresh produce directly from the farmer

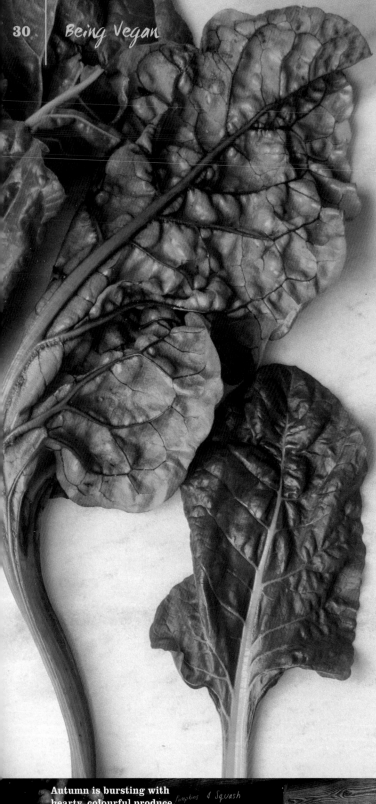

themselves to the types of dishes that will make you feel best at that point in the year – butternut squash and blackberries make warming casseroles, curries, crumbles and pies to see you through cold autumns, while beetroot, rocket and asparagus make light dishes perfect for warm spring days. Search online for recipes for the season, and you'll find all the inspiration you need.

To take things to the next level, why not consider growing your own produce? Whether you've got an allotment, a spare patch of soil in the garden or one sunny spot on the kitchen counter, you'll always be able to find something that's happy to grow there. Seed packets contain all the information you need about the best months to plant and harvest, and there are plenty of books and websites with helpful advice if you're new to gardening. By growing your own food, you're returning to a practice that kept your ancestors alive, and you have complete control over the conditions. If you have a glut of tomatoes or courgettes one summer, share them with friends, and encourage them to have a go themselves.

Eating locally and seasonally isn't always possible, of course, but there are very simple steps that you can take to return to a more traditional and sustainable way of eating. Make the changes that suit you and your lifestyle, and try not to feel guilty if you give in and end up buying a punnet of imported raspberries in January; strive for awareness and improvement, not perfection. Every time you *are* able to choose local and seasonal food, remember you're doing your bit for farmers, the environment, your wallet and of course your taste buds.

Autumn is bursting with hearty, colourful produce like squashes and pumpkins

Find space in an allotment or community garden, and you can grow your own food

Seasonal food at your fingertips

Eating seasonally and locally is a traditional way of life, but there's now technology available to make it easier. Here are a few apps and websites that will help you to locate farmer's markets and work out what's in season:

- *Seasons* This app lists the natural growing seasons and import seasons of hundreds of different kinds of produce, as well as markets around the world.

- *Seasonalfoodguide.org* This website will tell you which produce is in season in every US state.

- *Eatseasonably.co.uk* This site locates markets, restaurants and cafés that sell or cook with seasonal produce.

Spring

Blood oranges Rhubarb
Elderflower Alphonse mango
Gooseberries Apricots
Artichokes Cauliflower **Celery**
Asparagus **Wild leaf garlic**
Radishes **Chicory** Hispi cabbage
Jersey royal potatoes Purple
sprouting broccoli **Rocket**
Spring onion **Broad beans**
Leeks **Morels**
Spinach **Peas**
Rosemary Oregano **Tarragon**
Chives **Basil** Chervil **Coriander**
Marjoram **Bay** Flat-leaf parsley
Thyme Dill

Summer

Strawberries Cherries
Blackcurrants Peaches
Plums Blackberries
Rhubarb Gooseberries
Melons Grapes **Raspberries**
Pears **Greengages**
Elderflower **Apricots**
Redcurrants **Nectarines**
Blueberries **Figs** Damsons
Broad beans Courgettes
Chard Radishes **Runner beans**
Peppers **Cucumbers** Rocket
Aubergines Asparagus **Potatoes**
Borlotti beans Peas Fennel
Sweetcorn **Samphire** Spring
onions **Tomatoes**
Marjoram Chives **Flat-leaf
parsley** Thyme **Basil** Bay
Chervil Tarragon **Mint**
Sage **Coriander** Dill
Oregano Rosemary

Autumn

Apples Blueberries
Blackberries Piel de sapo
Victoria plums Cranberries
Grapes Quince **Nectarines**
Elderberries **Figs**
Pears **Clementines**
Aubergines Butternut squash
Leeks Swede **Carrots** Celeriac
Cavolo nero Celery **Pumpkin**
Courgettes **Brussels sprouts**
Fennel **Jerusalem artichokes**
Parsnips **Kale** Tomatoes
Peppers Cabbages **Radishes**
Rocket **Potatoes** Onions
Turnips
Basil Chives **Flat-leaf parsley**
Sage **Mint** Marjoram **Thyme**
Bay **Oregano** Rosemary

Winter

Pomegranates Clementines
Blood oranges Quince
Cranberries Rhubarb
Artichokes Leeks **Potatoes**
Brussels sprouts **Butternut
squash** Cauliflower **Celeriac**
Chicory **Swedes** Cavolo nero
Cabbage Celery **Watercress**
Spinach **Kale** Broccoli **Turnips**
Jerusalem artichokes
Parsnips **Onions**
Bay Rosemary **Sage**

● **Fruit**   ● **Veg**   ● **Herbs**

*Based on UK seasonality. Produce elsewhere will vary

Granola Bars

10
SERVINGS

10-15 mins
COOK TIME

20 mins
PREP TIME

1 hr
CHILL TIME

INGREDIENTS

- 300 g | 10½ oz | 2 cups rolled oats
- 150 g | 5⅓ oz | ½ cup maple syrup
- 75 g | 2½ oz | ½ cup tahini
- 65 g | 2⅓ oz | ¼ cup organic peanut butter
- 35 g | 1¼ oz | ¼ cup almonds, crushed
- 30 g | 1 oz | ½ cup pumpkin seeds
- 15 g | ½ oz | ¼ cup sunflower seeds
- 40 g | 1⅓ oz | ¼ cup raisins
- 40 g | 1⅓ oz | ¼ cup sultanas

RECIPE

1 Pre-heat the oven to 180°C (160°C fan) | 350°F | gas 4.

2 On a baking tray, toast the oats in the oven for 10-15 minutes, until golden brown.

3 Line an 20x20cm | 8x8" baking tin with parchment paper and set aside.

4 Warm the maple syrup, tahini and peanut butter in a saucepan over very low heat.

5 Meanwhile, using a mortar and pestle, carefully crush the almonds into 2-3 pieces.

6 Once the oats are toasted, add to the saucepan and combine well.

7 Fold in the almonds, sunflower seeds and pumpkin seeds, and combine well. Then, add the raisins and sultanas.

8 Transfer to mixture to the lined baking tray and press it firmly into place.

9 Refrigerate for about 1 hour, until firm. Then, cut into 10 bars and serve or store.

FLAVOUR VARIATIONS

A few simple tweaks can transform these granola bars into whatever flavours take your fancy

Granola bars are a great way to use up any dried fruit that you may have leftover in your cupboards – simply mix and match what you have available to make up the total amounts of fruit and nut. If you've got mixed peel left over from the festive season, try making a zesty version by adding that along with 1-2 tsp of grated orange or lemon zest to the mixture. Or snip a handful of chewy dried apple slices into small chunks and add ½ -1 tsp cinnamon for a warming autumnal brunch bar. You could also create some more indulgent oaty treats by replacing the nuts and seeds with some vegan chocolate chips or cacao nibs and some chopped stem ginger for sticky sweetness.

Buddha Bowl

2
SERVINGS

20 mins
PREP TIME

35 mins
COOK TIME

INGREDIENTS

- 1 small head of broccoli
- 1 sweet potato
- 1 red onion
- 10 mushrooms
- Olive oil, to drizzle and fry
- 1x 400 g | 14 oz tin chickpeas
- 1 tbsp paprika
- ½ tbsp turmeric
- ½ tbsp garlic powder
- ¼ tsp salt
- ¼ tsp pepper
- 100 g | 3½ oz | ½ cup quinoa
- 2 handfuls baby spinach, roughly chopped
- 2 handfuls cabbage, roughly chopped
- 1 avocado, chopped
- 75 g | 2½ oz | ½ cup shredded pickled beetroot
- Sunflower seeds, to garnish
- Cress, to garnish
- ½ lemon, sliced into wedges, to serve

RECIPE

1. Preheat the oven to 200°C (180°C fan) | 400°F | gas 4.

2. Remove large stems from the broccoli and chop roughly into small florets. Then, chop the sweet potato into slices and red onion into wedges. Roughly chop the mushrooms.

3. Arrange the sweet potato and red onion on a baking tray and drizzle with olive oil. Bake for 10 minutes.

4. Flip the sweet potato and red onion over. Then, add the broccoli and mushroom to the tray. Drizzle with olive oil and bake for another 8-10 minutes.

5. Meanwhile, drain the chickpeas and rinse thoroughly with cold water. In a mixing bowl, combine the chickpeas with paprika, turmeric, garlic powder, salt and pepper.

6. Warm 2 tsp olive oil over medium heat in a frying pan. Add the chickpeas and cook for 5-7 minutes. Set aside.

7. Meanwhile, rinse the quinoa. Then, add to a saucepan and cover with 300 ml | 10 fl oz | 1¼ cups cold water. Cook over medium heat, bringing to a rolling boil for about 15 minutes, until the water has evaporated and the quinoa has doubled in size.

8. Once cooked, wash thoroughly with cold water and set aside to cool.

9. Roughly chop the spinach, cabbage and avocado. Drain the pickled beetroot.

10. Arrange all the ingredients in a bowl, squeeze over some juice from a lemon wedge and garnish with sunflower seeds and cress.

MIX IT UP

Buddha bowls are great for using up leftovers if you need to pick & mix a healthy lunch in a hurry

Fruit and vegetables

Root out any leftover salad leaves or forgotten fruit and veg that may be hiding in your fridge. You can simply chop them raw, or roast/fry/grill them with some herbs or spices to add a variety of different flavours.

Filling fibre

Incorporate at least one portion of grains or beans into your Buddha bowl. Not only do they taste great and add texture, these fibre-rich foods boost your gut health and help keep you feeling fuller for longer.

Protein power

Add a good source of protein to your bowl. This could be fried cubes of marinated tofu, the aforementioned beans, a selection of mushrooms (criminally underrated nutritional powerhouses) or a handful of nuts and seeds.

Hummus & Tabbouleh

SERVINGS	SOAK TIME HUMMUS	PREP TIME HUMMUS	COOK TIME HUMMUS	STAND TIME TABBOULEH	PREP TIME TABBOULEH

INGREDIENTS

For the hummus

- 400 g | 14 oz | 2 cups dried chickpeas
- 1½ tsp bicarbonate of soda
- 5 heaped tbsp tahini (as high quality as you can afford)
- 1 lemon, juiced
- 1 garlic clove, crushed
- Pinch of salt
- Extra virgin olive oil, to garnish
- Zaatar, to taste
- Pita bread, to serve

For the tabbouleh

- 100 g | 3½ oz | ½ cup giant bulgur wheat
- 4 bunches fresh flat-leaf parsley, finely sliced
- 1 bunch mint, finely chopped
- 2 medium tomatoes, finely chopped
- 1 cucumber, chopped
- 125 ml | 4 fl oz | ½ cup freshly squeezed lemon juice
- 4 tbsp extra virgin olive oil
- Salt and pepper, to taste

RECIPE

For the hummus

1. Wash the chickpeas thoroughly and leave in a bowl with double the volume of cold water. Add 1 tsp of bicarbonate of soda, stir and leave to soak for 10 hours or overnight.
2. Drain the chickpeas and rinse them again with cold water.
3. Fill a large saucepan with water and add the chickpeas and ½ teaspoon of bicarbonate of soda. Place on high heat and bring to the boil. Once boiling, cover the saucepan and let simmer for about 1 hour. Check regularly and remove any white foam.
4. To check if the chickpeas are cooked, crush one between your fingers. If it feels soft and smooth, then they are ready.
5. Once ready, stir briskly to loosen the skins and remove any that come off.
6. Drain the chickpeas and reserve some of the cooking water. Then, rinse thoroughly.
7. Place the chickpeas in a food blender and blitz for about 1 minute. Add the tahini, lemon juice, garlic and salt, then blitz again. Scrape the sides as necessary and continue blitzing until the mixture is creamy and smooth. If the mixture is too thick, add 1 tbsp of chickpea cooking water at a time, until the consistency is correct.
8. Arrange in a bowl, drizzle with extra virgin olive oil and sprinkle with zataar. Serve with a side of pita bread.

For the tabbouleh

1. Place the bulgur wheat in a bowl and cover with about 2½cm | 1" of water. Let sit for 30 minutes, until it has doubled in size.
2. Meanwhile, rinse the parsley in cold water and pat dry. Remove the stems, finely slice and place in a large mixing bowl.
3. Chop the mint, tomatoes and cucumber, and add them to the mixing bowl.
4. Drain the bulgur, gently squeezing out any excess water, and add it to the mixing bowl.
5. Dress with lemon juice, olive oil, salt and pepper and mix thoroughly. Adjust seasoning to taste.

Momos & Chutney

SERVINGS

PREP TIME

COOK TIME

REST TIME

INGREDIENTS

For the dough
- **250 g | 9 oz | 2 cups plain flour**
- **1 tbsp olive oil**
- **120 ml | 4 fl oz | ½ cup water**
- **Salt, to taste**

For the filling
- **1 cabbage, finely chopped**
- **1 onion, finely chopped**
- **1 carrot, finely chopped**
- **1 spring onion, finely chopped**
- **1 pepper, finely chopped**
- **3 cloves garlic, crushed**
- **2 tbsp olive oil, plus more for greasing**
- **1 tsp garlic powder**
- **1 tsp black pepper (or Sichuan pepper if you have it)**
- **1 tsp soy sauce**
- **Salt, to taste**

For the chutney
- **2 tomatoes**
- **3 red chillies, dried**
- **3 tsp lemon juice**
- **½ tsp sugar**
- **1 tbsp black pepper (or Sichuan pepper)**
- **Salt, to taste**

To serve (optional)
- **1 spring onion, finely chopped**
- **½ tsp dried chilli flakes**
- **A drizzle of chilli oil**

RECIPE

1. In a bowl, combine the flour, oil and salt, and mix well. Slowly add the water and knead to make a firm dough.

2. Cover with a damp cloth and set aside for 30 minutes.

3. Meanwhile, prepare the chutney. Fill a saucepan half-full with water. Place over medium heat and bring to the boil.

4. Once boiling, add the tomatoes and dried chillies, and cook for about 10 minutes.

5. Strain the water and set the tomatoes and chillies aside to cool.

6. Once cool, cut the tops off the tomatoes and add to a blender, along with the chillies, lemon juice, sugar, pepper and salt. Blitz until a smooth paste forms. Set aside until it's time to serve.

7. Next prepare the momo filling. In a frying pan, heat the oil over medium heat. Add the crushed garlic and gently fry until it becomes fragrant.

8. Add the finely chopped cabbage, white onion, carrot, spring onion and bell pepper and cook for 3 minutes.

9. Add the garlic powder, black pepper and soy sauce, and cook for another 3 minutes, stirring well.

10. Once the dough has rested for 30 minutes, divide into 2 equal portions. Leave one portion under the damp towel.

11. Roll the second portion out onto a lightly floured surface until thin. While rolling, rotate, flip and flour the dough to prevent it from sticking to the surface.

12. Cut the dough into 10cm | 4" circles and place 1 tsp of filling in the centre of each circle.

13. Taking one edge of the dough, fold and pinch it together to form pleats, working all the way around. Then, pinch all of the pleats together in the centre, to seal.

14. Place the momos on a lightly greased plate and repeat steps 11-14 with the other half of the dough.

15. Heat some water in a steamer. Place the momos on a lightly greased steamer basket, leaving some space between each dumpling. Steam for 5 minutes, until the dough is no longer sticky to touch.

16. Serve the dumplings warm, scattered with the spring onion and chilli flakes and drizzled with chilli oil (if using), alongside the chutney for dipping.

FOLDING YOUR MOMOS

Get creative with your folding technique to
make a variety of neatly shaped dumplings

Cross shape

Place a spoonful of filling in the middle of one wrap. Bring opposite sides
of the dough together and pinch where they meet, rotate 90° and repeat.
Pinch the four loose 'cross' sections together to seal the dumpling.

Rosebud

Place 3 wraps in a row so that their edges overlap by about 2cm | 1".
Spoon some filling in a line across all three wraps, then fold the wraps
over to create a row of 3 semicircles. Take one end of the row and gently
roll up into a spiral.

Round twisted rope

Spoon some filling in the centre of one wrap, and place another wrap on
top. Pinch all the way around to seal the edges and then pinch and twist
thumbnail-sized sections of the edge, all the way around.

Soy Nuggets & Sweet Potato Fries

2

SERVINGS

1 hr

REST TIME

20 mins

PREP TIME

30 mins

COOK TIME

INGREDIENTS

For nuggets
- 2 vegetable stock cubes
- 475 ml | 16½ fl oz | 2 cups water, just boiled
- 90 g | 3 oz dried soya chunks
- 60 g | 2 oz | ½ cup plain flour
- 2 tbsp olive oil
- 120 g | 4¼ oz | 1 cup cornstarch
- 120 g | 4¼ oz | 1 cup panko breadcrumbs
- 3 tbsp sesame seeds
- 2 tsp paprika
- 2 tsp garlic powder
- 1 tsp salt
- 1 tsp pepper

For fries
- 2 sweet potatoes
- 2 tbsp olive oil
- 1 tbsp cayenne pepper
- 1 tsp salt
- 1 tsp pepper

To serve
- Condiments of your choice (see boxout)
- Salad leaves, to garnish (optional)

Light Bites

RECIPE

1 In a large bowl, mix the stock cubes with boiling water and stir well. Add the soya chunks and leave to sit for one hour.

2 Remove the chunks, and reserve ½ cup stock. Gently squeeze the chunks with paper towels, to remove excess water.

3 Preheat oven to 200°C (180°C fan) | 400°F | gas 4. Then, line a flat baking tray with baking parchment and set aside.

4 Combine the reserved vegetable stock, flour and olive oil in a bowl and whisk everything together until smooth.

5 Add the cornstarch to a shallow bowl and set aside.

6 In a separate bowl, stir together the panko breadcrumbs, sesame seeds, paprika, garlic powder, salt and pepper and set aside.

7 Take a soy chunk and toss it in the cornstarch bowl, to coat completely.

8 Next, dip it into the vegetable stock and flour mixture, using a slotted spoon.

9 Transfer the soy chunk to the bowl of breadcrumbs, and coat thoroughly. Repeat steps 7-9 with the remaining soy chunks.

10 Place the coated soy bites on the prepared tray and bake for 30 minutes, turning halfway through, until golden brown.

11 While the soy nuggest cook, peel the potatoes and cut them into 2½cm | 1" wide strips for chunky chips, or if you prefer skinnier fries, slice thinner strips about 1½ | ½" wide.

12 In a bowl, mix the potatoes with olive oil, cayenne pepper, salt and pepper.

13 Spread the fries onto a baking tray and cook for 20 minutes.

14 Serve the nuggets and fries together, with your choice of condiments and some salad leaves (if using).

MAKE YOUR OWN MAYO

With the help of a powerful blender, it's easy to whip up some dairy-free mayonaise. For more dip ideas, see page 48

- 120 ml | 4 fl oz | ½ cup soy milk
- 240 ml | 8 fl oz | 1 cup sunflower oil
- 2 tsp apple cider vinegar
- Pinch finely grated lemon zest (optional)
- Sea salt and white pepper, to season

1 Measure out your soy milk and set it aside to come to room temperature.

2 Once your milk is the same temperature as the oil, place the milk, oil, apple cider vinegar and lemon zest (if using) to a high-powered blender and pulse at a high speed until the mixture begins to emulsify and thicken.

3 Season to taste. Adjust the thickness if necessary by adding more milk if it's too thin, and more oil if it's too thick. Pulse again.

4 Store in an airtight container in the fridge. It will keep for 3-4 days.

Ratatouille

SERVINGS

30 mins
PREP TIME

45 mins
COOK TIME

INGREDIENTS

- 4 courgettes
- 2 aubergines
- 2 cloves garlic, crushed
- 2 large onions
- 1 yellow pepper
- 2 red pepper
- 4 large tomatoes
- 4 tbsp olive oil
- ½ tsp sugar
- 1 small bunch fresh basil, roughly chopped
- 1 small bunch flat-leaf parsley, roughly chopped
- Salt and pepper, to taste
- 4-8 slices of crusty bread, to serve (see below)

RECIPE

1 Cut the aubergines and courgettes into 2.5cm | 1" slices then deseed the peppers and cut them into bite sized chunks. Cut the onion into chunks too.

2 Score a cross in the bottom of each tomato and place them in a heatproof glass bowl. Cover them with boiling water and leave for a minute. Drain the water away and then when they are cool enough to handle, peel the skin off.

3 Cut the peeled tomatoes into quarters, deseed them and roughly chop the flesh.

4 Heat the oil in a casserole dish then add the onions. Cover the pot and leave on a gentle heat for around 10 minutes. Next add the aubergines, courgettes and cook for 3 minutes on a higher heat.

5 Add in the peppers, garlic, sugar and seasoning followed by half of the chopped basil and parsley.

6 Cook over a gentle heat for 20 minutes, then add in the tomatoes and cook for 10 more minutes.

7 Once ready, scatter the remaining basil and parsley on the top. Serve with a few slices of crusty bread (or make your own, see below) to mop up all the sauce.

INGREDIENTS

- 300 ml | 10 fl oz | 1¼ cup almond milk, unsweetened
- 3 tbsp pumpkin seeds
- 2 tbsp sunflower seeds
- 2 tbsp sesame seeds
- 50 g | 1¾ oz | ⅓ cup rolled oats, plus extra to decorate
- 1-2 tbsp maple syrup (to taste)
- 2¼ tbsp quick-rise yeast
- 3-4 tbsp vegan butter or baking spread, melted
- 275 g | 9½ oz | 2 cups bread flour (strong flour)
- 90 g | 3 oz | ¾ cup wholemeal flour, plus extra for kneading
- 2 tbsp ground flaxseed (linseed)
- 1 tsp fine sea salt
- Olive oil

Seeded loaf

14-15
SERVINGS

30-35 mins
PREP TIME

2½-3 hrs
REST TIME

35-40 mins
COOK TIME

1 Heat the milk in a small saucepan over a low heat until it is warmed through but doesn't boil. Pour the milk into a large bowl, then stir in the oats, maple syrup and yeast. Gently stir everything together an set aside for 5-10 minutes while you prepare the seeds.

2 Finely chop 2 tbsp of pumpkin seeds and 1 tbsp of sunflower seeds and add them to a small bowl with the sesame seeds. The remaining pumpkin and sunflower seeds will remain whole for decorating.

3 To the bowl with the milk and oats, stir in the melted vegan butter, bread flour, wholemeal flour, flaxseed and salt. Stir everything together with a wooden spoon until a dough starts to form.

4 Stir in the chopped seeds and sesame seeds. Take the dough on a clean, floured worktop and knead by hand for about 10 minutes. Alternatively, you can use a stand mixer with a dough hook attachment.

5 Coat the inside of a large bowl with some olive oil and place the dough into it. Turn the dough around in the bowl so it is evenly coated in the oil, then cover with cling film and a towel. Leave the dough to rest for about 90 minutes or until it's doubled in size. In the meantime, grease a loaf tin.

6 Once it's risen, knead the dough for a few more minutes on a clean, floured worktop, then shape it into a rough rectangle that will fit in your loaf tin. Place the dough in the tin, then cover with cling film and a towel and leave to rise again for about 60-90 minutes. It should reach about 2½cm | 1" above the top of the tin. Towards the end of this rising time, preheat the oven to 175°C (155°C fan) | 350°F | gas 4.

7 Sprinkle some oats and the remaining whole pumpkin and sunflower seeds over the top of the loaf, then bake in the middle of the oven for 35-40 minutes. Leave to cool for 10 minutes before turning out onto a wire rack and leave to cool for about 2 hours. Avoid the temptation to slice the bread until it's cooled!

Green Bean & Grilled Tofu Salad

4
SERVINGS

1 hr
REST TIME

20 mins
PREP TIME

25 mins
COOK TIME

INGREDIENTS

- 350 g | 12½ oz extra-firm, water-packed tofu
- 2 cloves garlic, crushed
- 2 tbsp light soy sauce
- 2 tbsp sesame oil
- 2 tbsp unseasoned rice vinegar
- 2 tsp brown sugar
- 200 g | 7 oz green beans
- 10 cherry tomatoes
- 10 yellow cherry tomatoes
- 1 sprig of thyme, leaves only
- 2 lemons, one zested and juiced, the other in slices

RECIPE

1. First, drain the tofu. Then place 5-6 paper towels onto a chopping board, lay the tofu on top of them and cover with 5-6 more paper towels.

2. Place a baking tray or another chopping board on top of the tofu. Then, place a heavy object, like a bowl, can or jar, on top of the tray. Let it sit for 1 hour.

3. Meanwhile, crush the garlic. Then, in a bowl, mix together the garlic, soy sauce, sesame oil, rice vinegar and sugar, to form a marinade.

4. One it has been pressed for an hour, cut the tofu into 5cm | 2" cubes.

5. Add the tofu to the marinade and leave it to marinate for 15 minutes on each side.

6. Remove tofu and set the remaining marinade aside for dressing.

7. Spray the tofu with cooking spray on all sides. Then, using a griddle pan over medium heat, grill the tofu for 3 to 4 minutes per side.

8. Meanwhile, fill a saucepan half-full with water and place over medium heat. Bring to the boil.

9. Rinse the beans under cold water and drain. Once water is boiling, add to the saucepan and cook for 3 minutes, until beans are tender. Drain and rinse them under cold water.

10. Chop the cherry and yellow cherry tomatoes into halves.

11. In a bowl, combine the tofu, green beans, tomatoes and thyme. Dress with lemon juice, and 1-2 tbsp of the leftover marinade.

12. Scatter with some lemon zest and serve immediately with lemon slices to garnish.

Pressing tofu helps to remove its excess water. Consider investing in a dedicated tofu press device to make this step easier.

Stuffed Butternut Squash

SERVINGS

PREP TIME

COOK TIME

INGREDIENTS

- **2 medium butternut squash**
- **2 tbsp olive oil**
- **170 g | 6 oz | ¾ cup quinoa**
- **350 ml | 12 fl oz | 1½ cups vegetable stock**
- **1 bunch curly parsley**
- **2 cloves garlic, minced**
- **1 tsp oregano**
- **1x 400 g | 14 oz can chickpeas**
- **1 orange, zest plus 1 tbsp juice**
- **1 handful fresh cranberries**
- **Salt and black pepper, to taste**

RECIPE

1 Preheat your oven to 200°C (180°C fan) | 400°F | gas 6. Use a sharp knife to carefully cut each butternut squash in half. Scoop out the seeds and place the halves on a baking tray, skin side down.

2 Drizzle with 1 tablespoon of olive oil and season with salt and pepper. Bake for 55 minutes until the squash is tender. Remove them from the oven and reduce the temperature to 180°C (160°C fan) | 375°F | gas 4.

3 While they are baking, put the stock in a saucepan and bring to the boil. Add the quinoa and leave to simmer for 12 minutes until most of the liquid has been absorbed.

4 Stir in the garlic, oregano, chickpeas, orange zest and 1 tbsp orange juice and cranberries. Then season to taste.

5 Remove from the heat and leave covered for 15 minutes, then use a fork to fluff it up and stir in some of the curly parsley.

6 Once the squash is cool enough to touch, scoop out a little of the flesh. You can either keep this for another dish, or stir it into your quinoa mix.

7 Stuff each squash with the quinoa mix and bake in the oven for 8 minutes. Drizzle with a little olive oil and sprinkle with more parsley to serve.

GET STUFFING

Vegetables and mushrooms can make handy vessels for all your favourite fillings. You could swap squash for...

Loaded potato skins

Bake a few large baking potatoes in the oven for about 45-60 minutes, then leave to cool. Slice them in half, scoop out some of the flesh (which you can mix into your filling) to create a well, and spoon the filling into it.

Peppers

Slice the tops off a few peppers and deseed them, but keep the tops. Rub a little oil over the skins, fill the peppers with your chosen filling, replace the tops and bake in the oven until the filling is cooked through.

Portobello mushrooms

Remove the stems, and marinade the mushrooms for a few minutes in a little olive oil and balsamic vinegar. Season well and fry them for 2-3 minutes on each side before adding the stuffing.

Spring Rolls

12 SERVINGS

15 mins PREP TIME

INGREDIENTS

For the marinade
- 1 tbsp lime juice
- 1 tbsp soy sauce
- ½ tbsp fresh ginger, grated

For the rolls
- ⅓ head red cabbage, finely julienned
- 5 spring onions, sliced into 5-7½cm | 2-3" long strips
- 1 cup pre-cooked rice noodles, sliced into 5-7½cm | 2-3" sections
- 1 small carrot, finely julienned
- ¼ cucumber, finely julienned
- 1 small handful baby salad leaves, such as rocket (optional)
- 1 small handful mint and/or coriander, leaves only (optional)
- 12 rice paper spring roll wrappers
- Soy sauce or tamari, to serve (optional)

RECIPE

1. In a large bowl, mix together all the ingredients for the marinade.

2. If you'd like to create neat and organised rolls, place the cabbage, spring onions, rice noodles, carrots and cucumber in separate bowls, divide the marinade between each one (a few teaspoons per bowl), then mix them well to coat.

3. Alternatively, for a more mixed-up filling, you can toss all the ingredients for the spring rolls – except the wrappers – together in a large bowl. Set aside for a few minutes to marinate while you make the sauce.

4. Next, dip the spring roll wrappers into warm water for 10-15 seconds until they become pliable.

5. For organised rolls, arrange small amounts of each filling (all the marinated ingredients plus the salad leaves and herbs, if using) across the bottom quarter of each wrap to form neat lines. For more mixed rolls, lay a few teaspoons of the filling in a line along the lower section of each wrap.

6. Roll the wraps over and around the filling, folding in the ends as you do to form a tight package. Be careful not to overfill the wraps as they may tear.

7. Serve with some soy sauce, or your choice of dip (see below) on the side.

DELICIOUS DIPS

Serve your rolls with a selection of sauces to give your crunchy spring rolls some extra flavour

Sweet chilli
- 1-2 tbsp chilli flakes, to taste
- 8 tbsp caster sugar
- 4 tbsp rice vinegar
- 2-3 garlic cloves, grated
- 240 ml | 8 fl oz | 1 cup water
- Salt & pepper, to taste
- ½ tbsp cornflour
- 2 tbsp water

Add the chilli flakes, sugar, vinegar, garlic and the water to a small saucepan and cook over a medium heat for a few minutes until the mixture starts to thicken. In a separate bowl, mix the cornflour and 2 tbsp water together until smooth, then add this to the saucepan and keep stirring until it's incorporated and starts to thicken more. Simmer until you reach your desired consistency (add some more water if it's too thick). Take off the heat and leave to cool before storing in an airtight jar in the fridge.

Peanut sauce
- 3 tbsp smooth peanut butter
- 2 tsp soy sauce (or tamari)
- 1-2 tbsp maple syrup
- 2-3 tsp rice vinegar
- 2 tsp lime juice
- 3-4 tbsp water

Mix together all the ingredients until smooth and even. Depending on how thick your peanut butter is, you may need to break it up a bit by stirring vigorously with a fork first. Store in an airtight jar in the fridge.

Ginger & soy sauce
- 4 tbsp soy sauce
- 4 tbsp toasted sesame oil
- 3 tbsp rice vinegar
- 2-3 tsp sugar
- 1 tbsp fresh ginger, grated
- 1 spring onion, finely chopped

Whisk together all the ingredients in a small bowl until the sugar has fully dissolved, and the ginger and onion are well distributed. You can add a little more sugar to taste. Store in an airtight jar in the fridge.

Light Bites

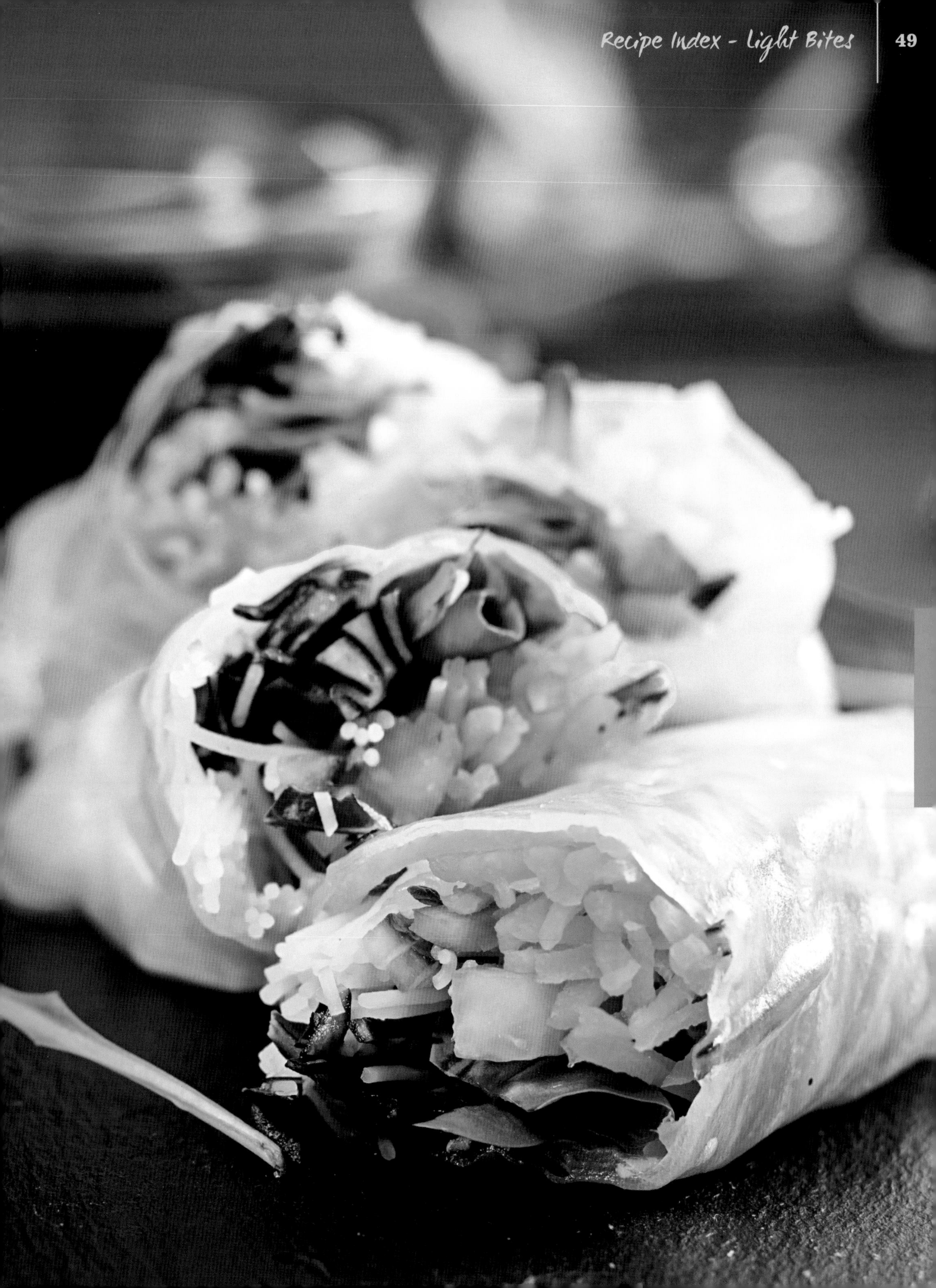

Pumpkin Soup

SERVINGS

PREP TIME

COOK TIME

INGREDIENTS

- 1 tbsp coconut oil
- 1 onion, chopped
- 2 cloves garlic, minced
- 1 tbsp ginger, minced
- 1 tsp thyme, leaves
- ½ tsp cayenne paper
- 415 ml | 14½ fl oz | 1¾ cups coconut cream
- 1 kg | 2¼ lb pumpkin, peeled and cubed
- 360 ml | 12½ fl oz | 1½ cups vegetable stock
- Salt and pepper, to taste
- Pumpkin seeds, to garnish
- Coriander leaves (optional), to garnish

RECIPE

1 Add the coconut oil into a large soup pot over a medium heat with the chopped onion, garlic and ginger, and gently fry for about 2-3 minutes.

2 Now add the thyme and cayenne pepper, and cook for a few minutes more, until the onions have softened.

3 Pour in the coconut cream, followed by the pumpkin and stock, then bring everything to the boil.

4 Simmer the soup for around 10 minutes, or until the pumpkin is cooked through. A skewer or knife should pierce one of the pumpkin cubes easily.

5 Remove the pot from the heat, then carefully use a handheld blender to blend the mixture until you have a smooth soup (or your desired consistency). If you don't have a hand blender, leave the soup to cool for 10 minutes and use a stand blender or a food processor.

6 Add salt and pepper, to taste, then sprinkle over pumpkin seeds and a few coriander leaves (if using) to serve.

WARMING WINTER FLAVOURS

Get your chef hat on and give this super soup your own signature twist by experimenting with other ingredients

You can replace the pumpkin in this recipe with other members of the squash family, like butternut squash or marrows. Experiment with other spices too: a little ground cinnamon for a hint of sweetness, ground ginger to boost the soup's warming zestiness, a sprinkling of chilli flakes if you like it spicy, or perhaps 1-2 pieces of star anise to give the soup fragrant aniseed notes. Add a little spice at a time, and build up slowly, tasting regularly to make sure you don't overdo it! Different winter herbs can also add an extra dimension of freshness to this hearty soup. Swap the thyme for rosemary, or drizzle each bowlful with some herb-infused oil before serving.

Breaded Tofu With Satay Sauce

SERVINGS

PREP TIME

COOK TIME

INGREDIENTS

For the tofu bites

- 3 tbsp vegan mayonnaise (see page 36, or use store-bought)
- 3 tbsp smooth peanut butter
- 1 cup panko breadcrumbs
- 2½ tbsp nutritional yeast
- 1 tsp garlic powder
- 1½ tsp salt
- 1½ tsp pepper
- 400 g | 14 oz extra firm tofu

For the satay sauce

- ½ small onion, finely chopped
- 2 cloves garlic, crushed
- 1 tsp sesame oil
- 1 tbsp light soy sauce
- 1 tsp tamarind paste
- 2 tbsp brown sugar
- 120 ml | 4 fl oz | ½ cup coconut milk
- 85 g | 3 oz | ⅓ cup peanut butter
- ½ lime, juice only
- 40 g | 1½ oz | ⅓ cup crushed peanuts
- 35 g | 1¼ oz | ¼ cup sesame seeds
- Fresh chives, chopped, to garnish
- ½ lime, sliced into wedges, to serve (optional)

RECIPE

1. Press the tofu for at least 30 minutes. Preheat your oven to 200°C (180°C fan) | 400°F | gas 6. Mix the mayonnaise with the peanut butter and set aside.

2. In a separate bowl, stir together the breadcrumbs, nutritional yeast, garlic powder, salt and pepper.

3. Pat the tofu dry with a paper towel, and cut into bite-sized chunks.

4. One by one, coat the tofu in the peanut butter mayo followed by the breadcrumb mix. You might need to lightly press the breadcrumbs in to make them stick.

5. Place the coated tofu on a lined baking tray and bake in the oven for 30 minutes.

6. Add the finely chopped onion to a saucepan with the garlic and sesame oil, then cook until the onion has softened slightly.

7. Next, add in the tamarind paste, brown sugar and coconut milk, and stir well. Now add the peanut butter and combine until smooth.

8. Remove the sauce from the heat and stir in the lime juice.

9. When ready to serve, sprinkle the crushed peanuts and sesame seeds over the sauce, and sprinkle over the chopped chives. Squeeze over the lime wedges, if using.

Light Bites

EXTRA SAUCES

Whip up some other dips to enjoy alongside these bite-sized breaded treats

Tomato ketchup

Mix together 8 tbsp tomato puree, 2 tbsp maple syrup, 1 tbsp apple cider vinegar and ½-1 tsp onion powder. Taste and season with salt and pepper. You can adjust the syrup/vinegar balance to your preference, if required.

Maple & mustard

Whisk together 2 tbsp American mustard, 2 tbsp wholegrain mustard, 2 tbsp maple syrup and 8 tbsp vegan mayonnaise, and season with salt and pepper to taste. Swap either mustard for other types if preferred.

BBQ sauce

Combine 8 tbsp vegan ketchup, 1½ tsp black treacle, 1 tbsp maple syrup, 1 tbsp apple cider vinegar, 1½ tsp soy sauce or tamari, 1½ tsp vegan Worcestershire sauce and ¼-½ tsp chilli sauce. Season to taste.

Grilled Vegetable Feast

4 SERVINGS

5-10 mins PREP TIME

40 mins COOK TIME

INGREDIENTS

- **3 courgettes**
- **1 aubergine**
- **6 cloves garlic**
- **3 cobs of corn**
- **8 shallots**
- **1 yellow pepper**
- **1 red pepper**
- **2-3 handfuls cherry tomatoes**
- **4 carrots**
- **1 tbsp fresh thyme leaves (or another herb of your choice, such as rosemary, or a mixture)**
- **Olive oil**
- **Salt and pepper, to taste**

RECIPE

1. Preheat the oven to 200°C (180°C fan) | 400°F | gas 6.

2. Chop all of the veg into large chunks then heat a griddle pan until it is extremely hot.

3. Drizzle the pan with a little oil. Next sear the vegetables in small batches until they begin to char.

4. Place the charred vegetables into a large roasting dish and then coat with a little more olive oil, season with salt and pepper, add the garlic cloves and sprinkle with thyme (or your chosen herbs).

5. Place the vegetables in the oven for 30 minutes, until everything is cooked through.

Vegetable Soup

SERVINGS — 4

PREP TIME — 10-15 mins

COOK TIME — 40 mins

INGREDIENTS

- Olive oil
- 1 large onion, peeled
- 1 whole cauliflower
- 3 carrots
- 2 potatoes
- ½ turnip, peeled
- 80 g | 3 oz | ½ cup frozen garden peas
- 1 litre | 2 pints | 4¼ cups vegetable stock
- 2 bay leaves
- Salt and pepper, to taste
- A few sprigs fresh flat-leaf parsley, leaves only

RECIPE

1 If you prefer your carrots and potatoes skinless, peel them, but it's fine to leave the skins on if you like.

2 Chop the onion, cauliflower, carrots, potatoes and turnip into chunks. You can dice them to whatever size you like depending on how chunky you like your soup – the smaller the pieces, the faster it will cook.

3 Heat a little oil in a large saucepan, then add the onions and cook over a medium heat until they begin to soften.

4 Add the carrots, potatoes and turnip and cook for another 2-3 minutes.

5 Next add the cauliflower florets to the pan, followed by the frozen peas, vegetable stock and bay leaves.

6 Bring to the boil and then simmer gently for 30-40 minutes. Once everything is cooked, taste and add seasoning as required.

7 Remove the bay leave and serve with a sprinkling of fresh parsley.

SEASONS' EATINGS

This recipe is incredibly flexible. You can adapt the soup throughout the year to enjoy which vegetables are at their best

Autumn & Winter

Try adding diced butternut squash, cabbage, celeriac, leeks, kale, pumpkin or parsnip, flavoured with parlsey, chives, sage, thyme, oregano or rosemary.

Spring & summer

Try adding chunks of asparagus, beans, courgette, green beans, new potatoes or tomatoes, flavoured with rosemary, basil, chives, coriander or mint.

Main Meals

Courgetti Bolognese

SERVINGS — 4

PREP TIME — 15 mins

COOK TIME — 30 mins

INGREDIENTS

- Olive oil
- 1 large onion, finely chopped
- 2 cloves garlic, minced
- 8 courgettes
- 450 g | 16 oz | 2 cups Quorn mince, or your favourite mince substitute
- 60 ml | 2 fl oz | ¼ cup vegan red wine
- 2 bay leaves
- 540 g | 19 oz | 2 cups passata
- 80 g | 2⅔ oz | 1 cup mushrooms, finely diced
- Salt and pepper, to taste
- Yeast flakes, to garnish
- Plum or cherry tomatoes, sliced, to garnish
- Fresh basil, to garnish

RECIPE

1 Heat a little oil in a saucepan and cook the onion and garlic over a medium heat until the onion begins to soften.

2 Next add the mushrooms and mince and cook for 2-3 minutes. Now add the red wine, bay leaves and passata and bring the mixture to a gentle simmer.

3 Leave to cook gently for around 30 minutes. Add more red wine if you'd like a richer sauce or use some water if it becomes a little dry.

4 While the sauce cooks, use a spiralizer to make the 'courgetti'. If you don't have a spiralizer you can use a julienne peeler to carve straight strands of the courgettes, or use a regular peeler to create thick, flat strands like tagliatelle.

5 When the bolognese sauce is almost ready, taste it and season if required.

6 Boil the courgetti in salted water for about 3 minutes, until it's heated through but still holds its shape. Alternatively, you can dry fry the courgetti for a couple of minutes.

7 Drain and serve the courgetti with a generous spoonful of the bolognese. Garnish with some fresh cherry tomatoes, a sprinkle of yeast flakes and a sprig of basil or two.

BEYOND COURGETTI

Mix up your routine by switching your regular pasta for extra nutritious fruit and veg

The spiralizer is a handy kitchen gadget to create spaghetti-like strands of fruit and vegetables. It's a great way of sneaking extra veg onto kids' plates, and making meals more colourful. Celeriac and swede are a good place to start, but you can make some really vibrant dishes with beetroot, carrot and squash. You can also make amazing curly fries by spiralizing a few potatoes and frying them. The extra surface area makes them super-crispy!

Try adding raw spiralized veg like cucumber to mix up the texture of salads, too. And don't stop at savoury ingredients either – you can spiralize hard fruits like apples and pears. For a delicious dessert, why not make a plate of fresh and crunchy sweet apple 'spaghetti', sprinkled with warming cinnamon and a dollop of vegan ice cream?

Sweet Potato and Chickpea Curry

6
SERVINGS

20 mins
PREP TIME

35-40 mins
COOK TIME

INGREDIENTS

- Olive oil
- 2 onions
- 3 tbsp rogan josh curry paste (see below, or use ready-made)
- 1 fresh chilli
- 3 sweet potatoes, peeled
- 1x 400 g | 14 oz tin chickpeas
- 1x 400 g | 14 oz tin chopped tomatoes
- 230 ml | 7¾ fl oz | 1 cup water
- 2 tbsp fresh ginger, grated
- 400 ml | 13½ fl oz | 1⅔ cups coconut milk
- 1 bunch fresh coriander, chopped

To serve
- Cooked basmati rice
- Steamed broccoli
- 1 lime, sliced into wedges
- A few sprigs fresh mint (optional)

RECIPE

1 Heat round 2 tbsp of oil in a large saucepan, then finely slice the onion before adding to the pan along with the curry paste. Cook for 10 minutes until the onion is soft and beginning to turn golden.

2 Finely chop the chilli – remove the seeds first if you'd prefer a more mild curry. Now chop the peeled sweet potato into rough 2cm | 1" chunks.

3 Add the chilli, ginger, and sweet potato to the onion mix followed by the drained chickpeas, and cook for 5 minutes.

4 Next add the chopped tomatoes and water then bring to the boil. Simmer for 10 minutes with a lid on, then remove it and cook for a further 15 minutes. If the sauce hasn't thickened much or the sweet potato isn't cooked through, keep it on the heat, uncovered, for a little longer.

5 Stir on the coconut milk and cook the curry for 5 more minutes.

6 Scatter with coriander and serve the curry with some rice and broccoli, plus a few sprigs of mint (if using) and a couple of lime wedges to squeeze over the top.

MAKE YOUR OWN CURRY PASTE

With a little help from a food processor, you can whip up a simple rogan josh paste in no time

Ingredients
- 1 tsp cumin seeds
- 1 tsp coriander seeds
- ½ tsp black peppercorns
- 1 clove garlic, peeled
- Fresh ginger, 2½cm | 1" piece, peeled
- 75 g | 2½ oz roasted red peppers (from a jar or roast your own), roughly chopped
- 1½ tsp sweet paprika
- ½ tsp smoked paprika
- 1 tsp garam masala
- ½ tsp turmeric
- ¼-½ tsp cardamom
- 3 tsp groundnut oil or vegetable oil
- 3 tsp tomato puree
- ½-1 red chilli (depending on how spicy you like it), roughly chopped
- Pinch sea salt

Method

1 Toast the cumin seeds, coriander seeds and black peppercorns in a dry pan over a medium-high heat for a couple of minutes until they become aromatic. Keep an eye on them to avoid burning, then remove from the heat.

2 Grind the toasted spices in a food processor (or with a pestle and mortar) until they are a fine powder.

3 Add the rest of the ingredients to the processor (or mortar) and keep grinding until everything comes together to form a smooth paste.

4 The paste will keep for a couple of months in an airtight jar stored in the fridge. Alternatively you can freeze individual tablespoon-sized portions, ready to add to the pan from frozen.

Yaki Soba

SERVINGS

PREP TIME

COOK TIME

INGREDIENTS

- 280 g | 10 oz soba noodles
- 1-2 tbsp toasted sesame oil
- 1 onion, finely diced
- 140 g | 5 oz | 1 cup shiitake mushrooms, caps only, thinly sliced
- 1 head sweetheart cabbage, or 2 small heads bok choy, shredded or finely sliced
- 2 medium carrots, julienned
- 3 tbsp soy sauce
- 3 tbsp rice wine vinegar
- 3 tbsp mirin
- 1 tsp fresh ginger, grated
- 1 clove garlic, minced
- 1-2 tbsp sesame seeds, to garnish

RECIPE

1. If you're using fresh soba noodles, you can skip this first step. If you're using dried soba noodles, cook them according to the packet instructions, then drain and rinse them in cold water to stop them cooking further. Toss them with a little oil to keep them from sticking together too much, and set aside.

2. Heat the oil in a large wok over a medium-high heat and fry the diced onion together with the sliced mushrooms until the onion starts to go translucent.

3. Turn the heat up to high and stir-fry the cabbage (or bok choy) and carrots for around 5 minutes until they are tender.

4. In a small bowl, whisk the soy sauce, vinegar, mirin, ginger and garlic together.

5. Add the soba noodles to the wok followed by the sauce and stir everything together.

6. Continue stir-frying for a couple of minutes until the noodles have heated through, and the vegetables have cooked and softened to your preference.

7. Serve each plate of noodles piping hot, sprinkled with sesame seeds.

Red Thai Curry

4-6 SERVINGS

20 mins PREP TIME

20-30 mins COOK TIME

INGREDIENTS

- 200g | 7 oz firm tofu, sliced into bite-sized cubes
- 2 tbsp soy sauce
- 1 tbsp fresh lime juice
- 1 tbsp olive oil
- 2 tbsp red curry paste
- 1 onion, chopped
- 1 thumb-sized piece of fresh ginger, peeled and grated
- 2 cloves garlic, minced
- 3-4 large tomatoes, roughly chopped
- 1 yellow pepper, diced
- ½ butternut squash, diced
- 1 aubergine, diced
- 1 courgette, diced
- 1x 400 ml | 13½ fl oz tin coconut milk
- 120 ml | 4 fl oz | ½ cup water
- A few sprigs fresh coriander, to garnish
- Cooked jasmine rice, to serve

RECIPE

1 In a bowl, toss the tofu cubes together with the soy sauce and 1 tbsp lime juice and set aside to marinade.

2 Heat the oil in a large pan over a medium-high heat, add the curry paste and cook until the aromas are released.

3 Add the chopped onion to the pan and continue to cook until it softens – about 5 minutes. Then add the ginger and garlic and cook for a further minute or so.

4 Next add the tomatoes, pepper, squash, aubergine and courgette to the pan and stir until they are evenly coated in the paste and oil.

5 Add in the tofu cubes and the marinade, then pour in the coconut milk and water and stir everything together.

6 Gently simmer the curry until the chunks of squash are tender and can be pierced easily with a knife. You might need to add a little extra water or coconut milk if it dries out.

7 Garnish the curry with some coriander leaves and serve with a side of jasmine rice.

Ultimate Burger

2 SERVINGS

25-35 mins — PREP TIME

8-35 mins — COOK TIME

INGREDIENTS

For the burgers:
Makes 12 (remaining burgers can be frozen)

- 145 g | 5 oz | 1 cup cashews or almonds
- 170 g | 6 oz | 3 cups cooked black beans or kidney beans
- 190 g | 6¾ oz | 1½ cups cooked rice (either white or brown)
- 40 g | 1½ oz | ¼ cup ground linseed (flaxseed)
- 120 ml | 4 fl oz | ½ cup water
- 15 g | ½ oz parsley, finely chopped
- 165 g | 5¾ oz carrots, finely grated
- 25 g | 1 oz | ¼ cup spring onions, finely chopped
- 100 g | 3¾ oz | 1 cup breadcrumbs
- Salt and pepper, to taste
- 1 tbsp paprika
- 1-2 tsp chilli powder (optional)
- Olive or vegetable oil (if frying)

For the avocado relish:
- 2 medium fresh avocados, skin and stones removed
- 1 lime, juice only
- ½-1 chilli pepper, chopped (seeds removed if preferred), finely diced
- 4-6 radishes, finely diced
- 4-6 pickled jalapeño slices, finely diced
- 1 small handful coriander leaves, finely chopped
- Salt and pepper, to taste

To serve:
- 2x vegan burger buns
- 1 pepper, skin roasted and sliced in half (or use ready-roasted slices)
- 1 handful cherry tomatoes, sliced
- 2-4 lettuce leaves
- 2-4 tbsp red onion chutney (see opposite page, or use ready-made)
- Chips (see right)

RECIPE

1 For the avocado relish, mash the avocado flesh into a puree with a fork or blender. Combine this with the remaining relish ingredients in a bowl. Mix well and set aside.

2 To make the burgers, mix the ground linseed and water together in a small bowl and set aside.

3 Add the cashews to a food processor and pulse until they are breadcrumb-sized. Add the rice and beans to the food processor and pulse a few times until the mixture forms a paste, but with some small chunks of beans still visible.

4 Pour the cashew, rice and bean mixture to a large mixing bowl. Add the linseed paste along with the remaining burger ingredients and stir everything together well.

5 Take about ½ cup of the mixture, roll it into a ball with your hands. Place it on a chopping board or baking sheet and flatten with the palm of your hand to form a patty about 2cm | ¾" thick. Repeat this step for the rest of the burger mixture. Freeze the remaining patties for next time.

5 The burgers can be fried, barbecued (step 6) or baked (step 7). To fry: heat some oil in a pan and cook the patties over a medium heat for about 4-5 minutes each side.

6 To barbecue: brush the grill with some oil and cook on a medium-high heat for 4 minutes each side.

7 To bake: preheat the oven to 175°C (160°C fan) | 350°F | gas mark 4 and place the burgers on a baking sheet for 35 minutes, flipping them half way through.

8 To assemble each burger, spread some relish on the lower bun, stack a lettuce leaf, the burger, chopped tomatoes, half the grilled pepper, a dollop of onion chutney, more relish and another lettuce leaf before topping with the other bun. Serve with a side of your favourite fries and dig in!

Perfect oven chips

10 mins — PREP TIME

15-20 mins — COOK TIME

Ingredients
- Around 100g | 3½ oz potatoes* per person, either floury or sweet
- A drizzle of olive or vegetable oil
- Salt and pepper, to taste
- Herbs and spices (optional**)

> * You can also branch out and try other veg – like celeriac, parsnips and carrots – to mix things up a bit.
>
> ** Try experimenting with different herbs and spices. Add rosemary for a fragrant flavour, a little paprika for sweet smokiness, or some garlic powder and chilli flakes for something more punchy! Once you've got a flavour combo you love, make a batch of it in a jar so it's ready to sprinkle whenever you feel like making fries.

Method

1 Line a large roasting tin with non-stick foil or parchment and preheat the oven to 200°C (180°C fan) | 390°F | gas mark 6.

2 Wash your potatoes (and peel them, if preferred) and slice them into 1cm | 0.4" thick sticks. Aim to keep them all the same size – this way they'll cook evenly. If you prefer a chunky chip, slice them thicker but remember they will need longer in the oven.

3 Place the chips on a plate and dab with some kitchen paper or a kitchen towel to help remove any excess moisture.

4 Pour the chips into a bowl, drizzle with oil (enough to coat the vegetables, but not so much that they're swimming in it) and season well. You could also add herbs and spices at this stage (see tip above). Toss everything together until all the chips look evenly coated.

5 Arrange the chips in a single layer on the roasting tin. If the tin is overcrowded it may be better to use a second one, or cook the chips in batches.

6 Bake them in the oven, taking them out to turn every 5 minutes. After around 15-20 minutes, they should be crisp and golden all over and tender in the middle. Remove from the oven and allow to cool slightly before serving.

Make your own onion chutney

12
SERVINGS

10-15 mins
PREP TIME

1 hr 30 mins
COOK TIME

Ingredients

- 2 tbsp olive oil
- 1kg | 2¼ lb red onions, finely sliced
- 200g | 7 oz | 1 cup dark muscovado or brown sugar
- ¼-½ tsp sea salt
- ¼ tsp freshly ground black pepper
- 120ml | 4 fl oz | ½ cup vegan-friendly red wine vinegar
- 2 tbsp balsamic vinegar
- 2-3 garlic cloves
- ¼-½ tsp chilli flakes

To store

- Sealable sterilised jar(s)

Method

1 Heat the oil in a large saucepan over a low heat and fry the onions for about 30 minutes until they're soft.

2 Add 2-3 tbsp of the sugar and turn the heat up to medium. Stir regularly and cook for about 8-10 minutes. Reduce the heat to low and add the rest of the sugar, along with the rest of the ingredients.

3 Bring to a gentle simmer and cook for 30-40 minutes, stirring occasionally to stop anything sticking to the bottom of the pan. The mixture should be caramelised and thickened.

4 Remove from the heat and spoon the chutney into a sterilised jar while it's still hot. It will keep for about 6-12 months.

Cauliflower & Bean Chilli

6
SERVINGS

20-30 mins
PREP TIME

1hr 30 mins
COOK TIME

INGREDIENTS

- 2 tbsp olive oil
- 1 tsp chilli powder (mild or hot, to taste)
- 1 tsp ground cumin
- ½ tsp Chinese five spice
- ½ tsp smoked paprika
- 1 large onion, diced
- 2 cloves garlic, grated or finely chopped
- 2 peppers (red or orange), deseeded and finely diced
- 2 medium carrots, finely diced
- 1-2 red chillies, to taste, sliced into rings (or deseeded and chopped, if preferred)
- 1 head cauliflower, florets diced into bite-sized pieces
- 1x 400 g | 14 oz tin kidney beans, drained and rinsed
- 800 g | 28 oz tomatoes, chopped (or 2x 400 g | 14 oz tins chopped tomatoes)
- Salt and pepper, to taste
- 1 small handful coriander, leaves only, to garnish
- 1 lemon, sliced into wedges, to garnish
- Cooked basmati rice, to serve

RECIPE

1. In a large pan over a medium heat, warm the oil and add the spices, onion and garlic and gently fry for about 10 minutes, stirring regularly. The onions should soften and the spices should become fragrant.

2. Add the peppers, carrots, red chillies and cauliflower florets to the pan, stir everything together and cook for 5 minutes more.

3. Next add in the kidney beans and tomatoes and bring the stew to a simmer. If you're using fresh tomatoes, you may need to add in up to 240 ml | 8 fl oz | 1 cup water during cooking depending on how much moisture they naturally contain.

4. Cover and leave the chilli to bubble away on a gentle simmer for 1-1½ hours, checking occasionally to give everything a stir. If you prefer a thicker stew, take the lid off for the final 20-30 minutes to allow the chilli to reduce.

5. When it's cooked, have a taste and season as required. Serve the chilli on a bed of fluffy basmati rice, scattered with a few fresh coriander leaves and a wedge of lemon on the side.

ADDING EXTRA DEPTH
Boost the flavour of your standard chilli with a few surprising optional ingredients

Cocoa or cacao

Chocolate and chilli make a fantastic odd-couple combination. Add couple of tablespoons of cocoa or cacao powder at step 2, or stir in a few squares of vegan chocolate, to give your stew an extra layer of flavour.

Coffee

Add a shot or two of strong, freshly brewed espresso (or a couple of teaspoons of dried coffee grounds) at step 3 to give your chilli some added earthiness and smokiness. It will also boost the meal's irresistible aroma.

Cola

Replace half a tin of the chopped tomatoes (or the cup of water) in step 3 with the same volume of cola, and leave the stew to reduce as required. The unique flavour and sweetness will take your chilli to another level.

Oatmeal Cookies

18-20
SERVINGS

40 mins
PREP TIME

10-12 mins
COOK TIME

INGREDIENTS

- 125 g | 4½ oz | 1 cup plain flour
- 200 g | 7 oz | 1 cup light brown sugar
- 115 g | 4 oz | ½ cup vegan butter or chilled dairy-free spread
- 140 g | 5 oz | 1½ cups rolled or porridge oats
- 1 tsp vanilla extract
- 1 tsp baking powder
- 3 tbsp golden syrup, maple syrup or apple sauce
- ½ tsp ground cinnamon
- ½ tsp salt
- Plant milk (optional)

RECIPE

1 Pre-heat the oven to 180°C (160°C fan) | 350°F | gas 4. Line 2 baking trays with baking parchment.

2 Cream together the vegan butter and brown sugar until smooth. Stir in the vanilla and the golden syrup, maple syrup or apple sauce.

3 In another bowl combine the flour, oats, baking powder, cinnamon and salt.

4 Add approximately one-third of the dry ingredients to the wet ingredients and gently mix with a wooden spoon. Repeat until all the ingredients are combined and a dough has formed. If the mixture is too dry and crumbly to roll into small balls, add a splash of plant milk.

5 Cover the dough with clingfilm and place in the fridge for at least 30 minutes.

6 Once chilled, take pieces of the dough and roll into evenly sized balls. Place the dough balls on the baking trays, leaving space between them so they can spread, and press down slightly.

7 Bake for 10-12 minutes until golden. The centres should still be slightly soft – they'll continue to firm as they cool.

8 Remove from the oven and leave to cool on the baking trays for 5 minutes before transferring to a wire rack to cool completely. Alternatively, enjoy them warm with a cup of tea or coffee.

FLAVOUR VARIATIONS

These delicious cookies can be adapted to include other sweet treats...

For oat and raisin

Soak 115 g | 4 oz | ¾ cup raisins for a couple of hours to plump them up, drain them and add at step 4, mixing well until they are evenly incorporated. For a bit of a boozy treat, soak the raisins in some rum instead.

For chocolate chip

Fold in 130 g | 4½ oz | ¾ cup vegan chocolate chips at step 4. Alternatively, you can press a few chips into each cut-out cookie at the end of step 6. Depending on your taste, you may prefer to omit the cinnamon.

For ginger cookies

Add ½-2 tsp ground ginger (to taste) at step 3. For extra fiery sweetness, fold in a small handful of crystallised ginger at step 4, or press a pinch of finely chopped stem ginger into the tops of each cookie at the end of step 6.

Raw Blueberry Cheesecake

10-12
SERVINGS

1-12 hrs
SOAK TIME

30 mins
PREP TIME

3+ HRS
CHILL TIME

Sweet Treats

INGREDIENTS

For the base
- **4 tbsp coconut oil**
- **175 g | 6½ oz | 1 cup Medjool dates, pitted**
- **70 g | 2½ oz | ½ cup raw almonds**
- **60 g | 2 oz | ½ cup raw pecans**
- **¼ tsp salt**

For the cheesecake
- **225 g | 8 oz | 1½ cups raw cashews, soaked overnight or boiled in water for an hour**
- **125 ml | 4½ fl oz | ½ cup maple syrup**
- **2 tbsp fresh lemon juice**
- **1 tsp vanilla extract**
- **125 ml | 4½ fl oz | ½ cup coconut milk**
- **1 tbsp coconut oil**
- **¼ tsp salt**
- **80 g | 2¾ oz | ½ cup frozen blueberries**

For decoration
- **1 handful fresh blueberries**
- **Desiccated coconut (optional)**

RECIPE

1 Bring together the ingredients for the base in a blender or food processor until they form a sticky mixture with pieces of almond and pecan still visible.

2 Firmly and evenly press the mixture into a 20x20cm | 8x8" baking tray lined with parchment. Place in the freezer to set.

3 Drain the soaked cashews and add them to the food processor along with the maple syrup, lemon juice, vanilla, coconut milk and salt. Blend until completely smooth.

4 Spoon half of the mixture into the baking tin and spread evenly over the base. Push a few frozen blueberries into the layer. Return the tin to the freezer.

5 Add the rest of the frozen blueberries to the remaining half of the mixture and blend until smooth and bright purple.

6 Pour the blueberry mix over the vanilla layer and spread gently. Firmly tap the baking tray on the counter a couple of times to even out the layers.

7 Freeze for at least 3 hours, preferably overnight. Once the cheesecake is completely set run a knife under hot water, dry it and use to cut the cheesecake into squares. Top with fresh blueberries and a sprinkling of desiccated coconut, if desired.

OTHER FRUITY FLAVOURS
Try out other flavours using a variety of frozen fruits

Summer berry
Replace the blueberries at steps 4 and 5 with a mixture of frozen summer fruits (you can often find pre-mixed packs in the frozen section of the supermarket). If the fruits are large, you can break them up in a food processor first.

Black Forest
Add 1-2 tbsp cacao powder to the base at step 1. Then pour 1-2 tbsp kirsch or cherry liqueur to the filling at step 3. Replace the blueberries with pitted frozen cherries at steps 4 and 5. Again, you may wish to blitz any large fruits.

Raspberry
Replace the blueberries with frozen raspberries at steps 4 and 5. You might want to add a little extra maple syrup if the rapsberries are tart. You could also sprinkle in some vegan white chocolate chips at step 4.

Energy Balls

10-14 SERVINGS

30 mins SOAK TIME

10 mins PREP TIME

1-2 hrs CHILL TIME

INGREDIENTS Pick your favourite flavour or make multiple batches

Chocolate

- 140 g | 5 oz | 1 cup mixed nuts (such as almonds, cashews, macadamias)
- 90 g | 3 oz | ½ cup dates, pitted and roughly chopped
- 90 g | 3 oz | ½ cup dried apricot, roughly chopped
- 75 g | 2½ oz | ½ cup raisins
- 2-3 tbsp desiccated coconut
- 2 tbsp cocoa or cacao powder
- 1 tbsp fresh orange juice

Tropical

- 140 g | 5 oz | 1 cup mixed nuts
- 90 g | 3 oz | ½ cup dates, pitted and roughly chopped
- 120 g | 4¼ oz | ¾ cup dried mango, roughly chopped
- 4 tbsp desiccated coconut, plus extra to coat
- 1 tsp lime zest
- 1 tbsp lime juice

Mocha walnut

- 70 g | 2½ oz | ½ cup mixed nuts
- 180 g | 6 oz | 1 cup dates, pitted and roughly chopped
- 30 g | 1 oz | ¼ cup raisins
- 50 g | 1¾ oz | ½ cup walnuts
- 2 tbsp cocoa or cacao powder, plus extra to coat
- 1 tbsp freshly brewed strong coffee or espresso

Blueberry

- 70 g | 2½ oz | ½ cup mixed nuts
- 180 g | 6 oz | 1 cup dates, pitted and roughly chopped
- 75 g | 2½ oz | ½ cup raisins
- 6 tbsp dried blueberries
- 1 tbsp lemon juice
- 1 tsp lemon zest

Peanut

- 140 g | 5 oz | 1 cups peanuts, raw and unsalted
- 180 g | 6 oz | 1 cups dates, pitted and roughly chopped
- 40 g | 2¾ oz | ¼ cup oats
- 2-3 tbsp maple syrup
- 1 pinch salt

Crunchy vanilla oat

- 80 g | 1⅓ oz | ½ cup oats
- 140 g | 5 oz | 1 cup almonds
- 180 g | 6 oz | 1 cup dates, pitted and roughly chopped
- ½-1 tbsp vanilla extract
- 1-2 tbsp maple syrup
- ¼-½ tsp cinnamon
- 1 pinch salt
- Chia seeds, to coat

RECIPE

1. Soak any dried fruit for your chosen flavour variation in warm water for 30 minutes to 1 hour or so, then drain and pat dry. This will rehydrate the fruit slightly to help it blend more easily.

2. Place all of the ingredients for your chosen flavour in a food processor and mix on a high speed. You may have to stop the processor and scrape the mixture away from the sides a few times to get everything mixed evenly.

3. The consistency of the mixture can vary depending on the combination of nuts you use, as well as natural variation in fruit moisture content. If the mixture is too wet, you can add a few more nuts. If it's too dry, slowly add a little more liquid (the fruit juice, coffee, or maple syrup, depending on your chosen flavour combination) or an extra date or two.

4. Use a dessert spoon to take chunks of the mixture and roll it into bite-sized balls. If the mixture is too sticky to handle, try wetting your hands before rolling, or put the mixture in the fridge for a while to set a bit first.

5. If your variation includes a coating ingredient (like coconut or cacao/cocoa powder) then roll each ball in the coating until covered.

6. Now put the balls in the fridge for 1-2 hours until they have firmed up. Store them in an airtight container in the fridge, ready for whenever you need a quick high-energy snack!

Sweet Treats

Raw Matcha Cake

8 SERVINGS

12 hrs SOAK TIME

10 mins PREP TIME

4 hrs CHILL TIME

INGREDIENTS

For the base

- 140 g | 5 oz | 1 cup almonds
- 20 dates, pitted
- 30 g | 1 oz | ¼ cup cacao powder
- 3 tbsp agave nectar
- Pinch sea salt

For the filling

- 750 g | 26½ oz | 5 cups cashews, soaked in water for 12 hours or overnight
- 225 g | 8 oz | 1 cup coconut oil, melted
- 240 ml | 8 fl oz | 1 cup coconut milk
- 120 ml | 4 fl oz | ½ cup agave nectar
- 7 tbsp lemon juice
- 2 tsp vanilla extract
- 2½-3 tbsp matcha powder (to taste), plus extra for dusting
- Pinch sea salt
- Edible flowers, to garnish (optional)

RECIPE

1. Put all of the ingredients for the base in a food processor and blitz until the mixture forms a fine crumble that sticks together.

2. Line a circular 25cm | 10" cake tin with greaseproof paper – a springform tin works best but a loose bottomed one will also do. Then pour the base mixture into the tin and compact it using your hand or the back of a spoon to form an even layer.

3. Next, make the filling. Drain the cashews and add them to a blender. Blitz at a high speed for a few seconds until it becomes nice and creamy.

4. Add the coconut oil, coconut milk, agave nectar, lemon juice, vanilla extract and a pinch of sea salt to the blender and keep mixing until everything is combined and the mixture is smooth.

5. Pour approximately ¼ of the filling mixture into a separate bowl and set aside. This will form your white middle layer.

6. Keep the remaining filling in the blender and add the matcha powder, mixing until the filling turns a lovely pale green.

7. Pour around half of the green filling over the base. Pick up the tin and give it a few firm taps against the worktop. This will help remove any air bubbles.

8. Gently spoon or pour the white filling on top of the green to create the middle layer.

9. Finally, pour the remaining green layer over the top. Give the tin a couple more gentle taps against the worktop.

10. Pop the cake in the fridge for at least 4 hours before serving.

11. Once set, dust the top of the matcha cake with a fine layer of matcha powder, and scatter with edible flowers (if using) for a vibrant green dessert.

Coconut Macaroons

14-16

SERVINGS

10-15 hrs

PREP TIME

12-15 mins

COOK TIME

INGREDIENTS

- 80g | 2¾ oz | ⅞ cups desiccated coconut (or 100g | 3½ oz | 1¼ cups coconut flesh, freshly grated)
- 125ml | 4½ fl oz | ½ cup coconut milk
- 1 tbsp coconut flour
- 2 tbsp maple syrup
- 1 vanilla pod, seeds scraped (or ½-1 tsp vanilla extract)
- 1 pinch salt

RECIPE

1 Preheat the oven to 180°C (160°C fan) | 355°F | gas 4, and line a large baking tray with baking parchment.

2 Add all the ingredients to a large saucepan and warm over a medium heat. Stir the mixture well and cook for around 5 minutes – the coconut milk should absorb into the coconut and flour, thickening the mixture. Remove the saucepan from the heat and leave to cool.

3 Once the mixture is cool enough to handle, spoon it into a piping bag with a large star-shaped nozzle and pipe 14-16 macaroons onto the baking sheet. Alternatively, you can scoop spoonfuls of the mixture and roll them into balls. Press each one onto the baking tray to form domes, leaving space between each one.

4 Bake in the middle shelf of the oven for approximately 12-15 minutes, until golden brown around the edges.

5 Remove from the oven and leave to cool completely before serving. You could also dip the base of each macaroon in some melted vegan chocolate for an extra indulgent treat.

Raw Chocolate Brownie

SERVINGS

PREP TIME

CHILL TIME

INGREDIENTS

- **450 g | 16 oz | 3 cups Medjool dates, pitted**
- **220 g | 7¾ oz | 1½ cups blanched hazelnuts**
- **6 tbsp cacao powder**
- **2 tbsp date syrup (or maple syrup)**
- **110 g | 4 oz | 1 cup goji berries, roughly chopped**
- **125 g | 4¼ oz | ½ cup crushed pistachio nuts**
- **100 g | 3½ oz vegan dark chocolate**
- **Pinch sea salt, to garnish**

RECIPE

1 Toast the hazelnuts in a dry pan over a medium-high heat (alternatively, roast them in a hot oven) for about 5 minutes or until golden and fragrant. Set aside to cool.

2 Once the hazelnuts are cooled, blitz them in a food processor until they form a crumbly sand-like mixture.

3 Add the dates and blend again before adding the cacao and date syrup. Blend further until everything is mixed together.

4 Pour the brownie mix into a large bowl, and mix in the chopped goji berries and crushed pistachios. Stir it together until everything is evenly distributed.

5 Press the mix into a baking tray and pop it in the fridge for 3-4 hours to set.

6 Once chilled, melt the chocolate and drizzle it over the top, chill again until the chocolate has set, then serve with a sprinkling of sea salt.

Blackberry & Almond cake

10
SERVINGS

20 mins
PREP TIME

90 mins
COOK TIME

INGREDIENTS

For the topping

- 3 tbsp dairy-free spread
- 85 g | 3 oz | ²/₃ cups plain flour
- 3 tbsp light brown soft sugar
- 3 tbsp agave nectar
- 2 tbsp flaked almonds

For the cake

- 250 g | 9 oz | 2 cups plain flour
- 2 tsp baking powder
- ½ tsp bicarbonate of soda
- 225 g | 8 oz | 1 cup caster sugar
- 100 g | 3.5 oz | 1 cup ground almonds
- 130 ml | 4.5 fl oz | ½ cup sunflower oil
- 1½ tsp vanilla extract
- ½ tsp almond extract
- 200 ml | 7 fl oz | ⁴/₅ cup soya milk
- 175 g | 6 oz | 1½ cup blackberries

RECIPE

1 Heat the oven to 180°C, Gas 4. To make the topping, rub the spread into the flour in a bowl using your fingertips. Stir in the sugar until well combined, then set aside.

2 For the cake, sift the flour, baking powder and bicarbonate of soda into a bowl, then stir in the sugar and ground almonds. Add the oil, vanilla extract, almond extract and soya milk. Gently fold through the blackberries to create a smooth mixture.

3 Spoon mixture into the prepared tin, smooth with a spatula and top with crumble mixture and flaked almonds. Cover with foil and bake for 1 hour. Remove foil and bake for a further 30 mins, or until an inserted skewer comes out clean.

4 Remove the cake from the oven and leave to cool in the tin on a wire rack.

Chocolate celebration cake

10
SERVINGS

40 mins
PREP TIME

35 mins
COOK TIME

INGREDIENTS

For the cake

- 325 g | 11.4 oz | 2²/₃ cups gluten-free plain flour
- 2 tbsp cocoa powder
- 250 g | 8.8 oz | 1¼ cups caster sugar
- 250 g | 8.8 oz | 1¼ light muscovado sugar
- 2 tbsp gluten-free baking powder
- 2 tbsp cider vinegar
- 2 tsp vanilla extract

For the filling

- 150 g | 5.3 oz | ²/₃ cup pure soya spread
- 4 tbsp icing sugar
- 2 tbsp cocoa powder
- 2 tbsp raspberry jam

For the ganache

- 200 g | 7 oz | 1 cup dairy-free dark chocolate, broken into squares
- 160 ml | 5.7 oz | ²/₃ cup coconut cream

RECIPE

1 Heat the oven to 180°C, Gas 4. Grease and line two 20cm cake tins with baking paper. Sift the flour and cocoa powder into a mixing bowl, then stir in the sugars and baking powder.

2 Mix the cider vinegar and vanilla with 400ml water, then slowly beat it into the flour mixture to make a batter (it will be quite runny). Divide the mixture evenly between the cake tins and bake for 35 mins until just firm and springy to the touch. Leave to cool in the tins.

3 To make the filling, mix together the soya spread, icing sugar and cocoa powder. Set aside. To make the ganache, melt together the chocolate and coconut cream in a bowl set over a pan of barely simmering water. When melted and smooth, leave to cool and thicken slightly.

4 Sandwich the cakes together with a layer of raspberry jam topped with the cocoa filling mixture. Drizzle the ganache over the cake, allowing it to drip down the sides. Decorate how you wish.

Pumpkin spice loaf

10
SERVINGS

20 mins
PREP TIME

70 mins
COOK TIME

INGREDIENTS

For the cake

- **170 g | 6 oz | 1 cup brown rice flour**
- **1 tbsp ground almonds**
- **1 tbsp coconut flour**
- **170 g | 6 oz | 1 cup coconut sugar**
- **1½ tsp cinnamon**
- **½ tsp nutmeg**
- **3-4 cloves**
- **1¼ tsp bicarbonate soda**
- **¼ tsp baking powder**
- **¼ cup unsweetened apple sauce**
- **60 g | 2 oz | ⅕ cup coconut milk yogurt**
- **1 medium ripe avocado, pitted**
- **230 g | 8 oz | 1 cup pumpkin purée OR butternut squash purée for a lighter colour**
- **2 tbsp maple syrup**
- **½ tsp vanilla paste**
- **3 tbsp dark chocolate chunks (optional)**

For the frosting

- **60 g | 2 oz | ⅕ cup coconut cream**
- **60 g | 2 oz | ⅕ cup coconut milk yogurt**
- **2 tbsp maple syrup**
- **2 tbsp coconut oil, softened**
- **1 tsp vanilla paste**
- **¼ tsp cinnamon (optional)**

RECIPE

1 Preheat the oven to 180°C/Gas 4 and grease and line a loaf tin with baking parchment.

2 Stir together the brown rice flour, almonds, coconut flour, coconut sugar, spices, bicarbonate of soda, baking powder and ¼ tsp salt.

3 Blend together the egg, milk yogurt, avocado, pumpkin purée or butternut squash purée, maple syrup and vanilla paste until smooth. Stir the wet ingredients into the dry ones and mix until combined. Stir through the chopped walnuts and the chocolate if adding. Pour this mixture into the loaf tin, smoothing down the top and bake for 1 hour or until cooked through. If the cake is browning too much halfway through cooking, place some baking parchment over the top and leave it to bake.

4 Beat together the frosting ingredients, then place in the fridge to thicken. Once the loaf is baked, leave to cool before spreading over the frosting.

Vanilla cake

10
SERVINGS

20 mins
PREP TIME

35 mins
COOK TIME

INGREDIENTS

For the cake

- **300 g | 10.5 oz | 2 ⅓ cup plain flour**
- **2 tsp baking powder**
- **175 g | 6 oz | 1 cup caster sugar**
- **130 ml | 4.5 fl oz | ½ cup sunflower oil**
- **2 tsp vanilla extract**
- **200 ml | 7 fl oz | ¾ cups almond milk**

For the icing

- **250 ml | 9 fl oz | 1 cup vegan whipping cream or thick coconut yogurt**
- **1 tbsp icing sugar**
- **4 tbsp raspberry jam**

RECIPE

1 Heat the oven to 180°C, Gas 4. Sift the flour and baking powder into a bowl, then add the sugar and mix well.

2 Pour in the sunflower oil and vanilla extract and mix well. Fold in the milk in 2 additions to make

3 Divide between the prepared tins and bake for 30-35 mins or until a skewer inserted in the centre comes out clean. Leave to cool.

4 Meanwhile, whip the cream or coconut yogurt and half the icing sugar to form soft peaks; set aside. Spread the jam on to one sponge, then spread the cream evenly over this. Top with the second sponge and dust with the rest of the icing sugar.

chocolate fudge

10
SERVINGS

15 *mins*
PREP TIME

24 *hrs*
CHILL TIME

Sweet Treats

INGREDIENTS

For the fudge

- **250 g | 8.8 oz | 1 cup coconut milk**
- **3 tbsp agave**
- **100 g | 3.5 oz | ½ cup natural nut butter**
- **500 g | 17 oz | 2 ½ cup 100% dark chocolate**
- **100 g | 3.5 oz | ²/₃ cups pistachios, chopped**

RECIPE

1 Pour the coconut milk, agave and nut butter into a pan over a low heat, stir and allow it to reach a simmer.

2 Put the chocolate, broken into pieces, into a glass bowl and pour over the mixture and stir until melted and thoroughly combined. Fold in the chopped nuts, keeping a few bits back to place on top.

3 Pour the mixture into lined tin and top with remaining nuts. Place in the fridge and allow to set – overnight if possible.

4 Remove the fudge from the tin and discard the cling film. Cut it into cubes.

Peanut butter brownies

14
SERVINGS

20 mins
PREP TIME

35 mins
COOK TIME

INGREDIENTS

For the brownies

- **275 g | 9.7 oz | 1 ½ cups dairy-free dark chocolate**
- **75 g | 2.6 oz | ¼ cup peanut butter**
- **300 g | 10.5 oz | 1 ½ cups caster sugar**
- **150 g | 5.2 oz | 1 ¼ cup flour, sifted**
- **1 tsp baking powder**
- **150 g | 5.2 oz | ¾ cups ground almonds**
- **175 ml | 6 fl oz | ²/₃ cups unsweetened soya milk**

RECIPE

1 Heat the oven to 180°C, Gas 4. Over a low heat, melt the chocolate with the peanut butter in a saucepan and stir to combine. Remove from the heat, then stir through the sugar and leave to cool slightly.

2 Fold in the flour, baking powder and almonds. Fold in the soya milk in 3 stages and mix until combined. Spread the mixture into the prepared tin and bake for 25-35 mins, or until the brownie has formed a crust but still feels a little soft in the centre. Cut into squares to serve.

Delicious Dinner Party

Cook up a storm in the kitchen and host a winning vegan dinner party

Hosting a dinner party can be stressful at the best of times, but never more so when your guests have varying dietary requirements. Blow the vegan sceptics away with this stunning three-course meal. Show your non-vegan guests that vegan food can be wildly creative and incredibly tasty.

Start with a drink

Thankfully there are many drinks to choose from that are suitable for vegans. Welcome your guests with a refreshing Hugo. Simple add 25ml | ⅞ fl oz of elderflower liqueur to a large wine glass, followed by a generous slug of prosecco, a few mint leaves and some slices of lime. Make a non-alcoholic version with elderflower cordial and soda water instead of prosecco. Pair a rich red wine with your rainbow lasagne and perhaps finish the meal with a coffee spiked with your favourite liqueur.

Pre-dinner nibbles

Any good host will make sure their guests are never left wanting, so to ensure you hold the perfect dinner party, provide some pre-dinner nibbles. For ease, simply cut up strips of carrots, cucumber, celery and peppers and serve them with a side of hummus. Or slice your favourite root vegetables as thinly as you can, drizzle them with olive oil and season before popping in the oven until crisp. Olives are always a winner too!

Purple Sushi

SERVINGS

PREP TIME

COOK TIME

Ingredients

- 250 g | 10½ oz | 1½ cups Thai purple gelatinous rice
- 590 ml | 20 fl oz | 2¾ cups water
- 60 ml | 2 fl oz | ¼ cup rice vinegar
- 3 tbsp agave syrup
- ½ tsp salt
- 4 nori sheets
- 1 large red pepper, julienned
- 3 carrots, julienned
- 1 cucumber, peeled and julienned
- 2 avocados, cut into thin strips
- ½ mango, cut into thin strips
- 4 tbsp vegan mayo (optional)
- 4 tbsp sweet chilli sauce (optional)
- Pickled ginger, to serve
- Vegan wasabi sauce, to serve
- Soy sauce or tamari, to serve

Method

1 Place the rice and water in a saucepan and bring to the boil. Now leave it covered to simmer for 15-20 minutes until it is fluffy and sticky. Put the cooked rice into a bowl to cool and set aside to cool.

2 While the rice is cooling, you can prepare the pepper, carrots, cucumber, avocados and mango for the filling if you haven't already.

3 Now add the rice vinegar, agave and salt to the rice and use a wooden spoon to mix through thoroughly.

4 Place the first sheet of nori on the bamboo sushi mat and spoon a quarter of the rice on the sheet leaving a 2½cm | 1" gap at one end. Make sure you press the rice down and try to make the layer relatively thin.

5 Now lay about one quarter of your filling ingredients in a row near the end where the rice goes all the way to the edge. Spoon over some vegan mayo (if using).

6 Next roll up the bamboo mat tightly starting at the end with the filling until everything is tightly rolled together. Remove the mat and cut into bite sized pieces using a sharp, wet knife.

7 Repeat with the rest of the ingredients and serve the sushi with some soy sauce, pickled ginger and wasabi.

Dinner Party

Rainbow Lasagne

INGREDIENTS

- 30 vegan lasagne sheets
- 2 cups almond milk
- 2 tbsp butter
- 1 vegetable stock cube
- 1 tbsp nutritional yeast
- Olive oil
- Salt and pepper (to season each filling, to taste)

For the beetroot
- 1½ kg | 53 oz beetroot, peeled and chopped
- 4 garlic cloves
- 1 tbsp thyme leaves

For the pumpkin
- 1½ kg | 53 oz pumpkin, peeled and chopped
- ½ tsp ground nutmeg
- ¼ tsp chilli flakes
- 4 cloves garlic
- 1 tsp peanut butter

For the spinach & 'ricotta'
- 500 g | 16 oz fresh baby leaf spinach
- 5 tbsp cashews, soaked overnight
- 1 tbsp pumpkin seeds
- 2 cloves garlic, minced
- 1 tbsp nutritional yeast
- ¼ lemon, juice only
- 2 basil leaves
- 1 tsp nutmeg ground

For the tomato sauce
- 680 g | 24 oz | 2½ cups passata
- 1 onion, finely chopped
- 3 cloves garlic
- ¼ tsp chilli flakes
- 1 tbsp thyme leaves
- 2 bay leaves
- 1½ cups hot water

For the mushrooms
- 700 g | 24 oz | 9 cups mushrooms

8 SERVINGS

12+ hrs SOAK TIME

50 mins PREP TIME

45-50 mins COOK TIME

Method

1 Preheat the oven to 200°C (180°C fan) | 400°F | gas mark 6. For the pumpkin layer, mix the pumpkin in a bowl with the nutmeg, garlic, sea salt, chilli and a drizzle of olive oil. In a separate bowl, mix together the ingredients for the roasted beetroot.

2 Spread the pumpkin on one baking tray and the beetroot mixture on another. Bake in the oven for 35 minutes.

3 While the vegetables roast, start the tomato sauce. In a medium saucepan gently cook the onion, garlic and chilli flakes in a little oil until soft.

4 Add the passata, thyme, bay, salt and hot water and simmer for 15-20 minutes. Remove from the heat and set aside.

5 When the pumpkin and beetroot are finished roasting, remove them from the oven (leave the oven on as you'll need it later). Leave the pumpkin to cool slightly before blending with the peanut butter until smooth. Set aside for later. In a separate bowl, blend the beetroot mixture until almost smooth. Set aside.

6 To make the 'ricotta', drain and rinse the cashews and pop them in the food processor. Add the pumpkin seeds and blend until smooth. Add in the garlic, nutritional yeast, lemon, basil, nutmeg and salt and pepper. Process until smooth. Add a little water if it's dry.

7 In a large pan, cook the spinach with the chilli flakes, salt and a drizzle of olive oil. Remove from the heat and once cool stir through the 'ricotta'.

8 In another large pan fry the mushrooms and thyme in olive oil until soft.

9 Season each filling to taste. Now it's time to assemble the lasagne. In a large, deep dish, arrange the ingredients in the following order, with a layer of lasagne sheets (LS) in between each mixture: ½ the tomato mix, LS, ½ the tomato mix, LS, the spinach mix, LS, the pumpkin mix, LS, the mushroom mix, LS, ¾ the beetroot mix, LS, then the rest of the beetroot followed by one final layer of lasagne.

10 In a small saucepan, make a roux from the flour and 2 tbsp of oil, then add the almond milk a little at a time until smooth. Add a vegetable stock cube and the nutritional yeast. Keep stirring until the mix begins to thicken.

11 Pour the vegan cheese sauce over the top of the lasagne and bake in the oven for

Raw Carrot & Pistachio Cake

14
SERVINGS

12+ hrs
SOAK TIME

45 mins
PREP TIME

4+ hrs
CHILL TIME

INGREDIENTS

- 370 g | 13 oz | 3 cups raw walnuts
- 150 g | 5 oz | 1½ cup desiccated coconut
- 90 g | 3 oz | ¾ cup coconut flour
- 70 g | 2½ oz | ⅓ cup coconut oil, melted
- 3 tbsp lemon juice
- 3 tsp vanilla extract
- 3 tsp ground cinnamon
- 2 tsp ground ginger
- ½ tsp ground nutmeg
- 1 lemon, zest only
- 525 g | 18½ oz | 3 cups Medjool dates, pitted
- 150 g | 5 oz | 3 cups carrots finely grated
- 200 g | 7 oz | 2 cups crushed pistachios
- Pinch fine sea salt

For the frosting:

- 150 g | 5oz | 1 cup raw cashews, soaked overnight
- 60 ml | 2 fl oz | ¼ cup unsweetened coconut milk
- 30 g | 1 oz | ¼ cup coconut oil, melted
- 3 tbsp maple syrup
- 2 tbsp lemon juice
- 1 tsp vanilla extract
- Pinch fine sea salt
- 50 g | 1½ oz | ½ cup crushed pistachios

Method

1. Pop the walnuts in a food processor and pulse them until they are finely ground. Then add the desiccated coconut, coconut flour, spices, salt, lemon zest and pulse a few more times until everything is combined.

2. Next add the coconut oil, lemon juice and vanilla extract and pulse again.

3. Turn the food processor on and add in one date at a time through the feed tube. Now tip the mixture into a large mixing bowl and fold in the crushed pistachios and grated carrot.

4. Press the mixture into two 15cm | 6" greased loose bottomed cake tins. Now pop the raw cakes into the freezer while you make the icing.

5. Put the cashews, coconut milk, melted coconut oil, maple syrup, lemon juice, vanilla and salt into a blender and blitz on a high speed until the mixture is smooth and creamy.

6. Remove the carrot cakes from the freezer, then spread half of the icing on one cake, place the other cake on top, then add the remaining icing. Sprinkle the remaining chopped pistachios on top.

7. Put the cake back in the freezer for around four hours before serving. Either serve frozen, or leave to thaw while you enjoy your main course, or for 15 minutes before serving.

Lifestyle & Sustainability

Are You Vegan Enough? **100**
Rebecca Greig

Being Vegan on a Budget **106**
Victoria Williams

The Power of Plant Protein **110**
Beate Sonerud

The Vegan Home **112**
Joanne Al-Samarae

Health & Beauty **114**
Alice Barnes-Brown

Fashion with a Conscience **118**
Joanne Al-Samarae

Fighting the Throwaway Culture **120**
Victoria Williams

Eco-Friendly Travel **126**
Joanne Al-Samarae

How to be a Globetrotting Vegan **130**
Alice Barnes-Brown

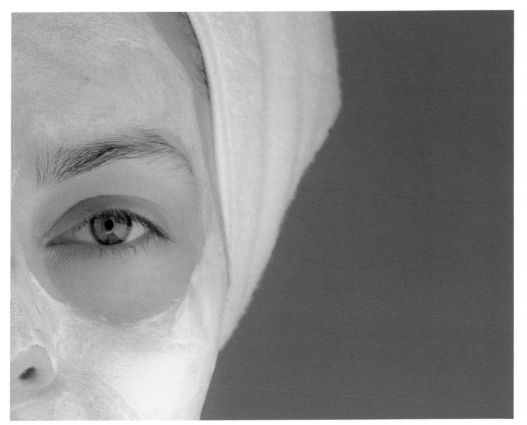

Are You Vegan Enough?

In our modern world where convenience is king, can anyone really be 100% vegan?

"Y ou're a bad vegan" is a phrase thrown around all too often by both non-vegans and vegans alike, but what makes someone a 'good' or 'bad' vegan and why? Should there be levels of veganism? And what gives people the right to judge if someone is vegan *enough*, and how are they measuring veganism? We didn't realise that we had to meet this vision of a vegan 'ideal' to call ourselves vegan, but many of us know all too well that there are those who think we do – and these people are typically quick to point fingers at anyone who doesn't live up to the seemingly ever-changing criteria.

As we know, being vegan is all about avoiding animal products, fighting against animal cruelty and helping the environment. Animal welfare is a topic that many people are highly passionate about, and vegans often get a bad name for

forcing their beliefs on the rest of society. Vegans also have a reputation of believing they are superior because of their strong views and willingness to fight for a better world. However, more often than not, the non-vegans are just as bad with their judgemental views on the lifestyle choices of others.

Here, we take a look at some points of debate surrounding veganism.

The pollination conundrum

Honey is all too often mistaken as being safe for vegans, however, for most it is not. When bees make honey they are making it for themselves, so when it is harvested by humans, the bee's health is sacrificed. Many vegans abstain from the consumption of honey to protect the bees, but are they being exploited in the production of other

Did you know

While they don't have pain receptors like animals, studies have shown that plants do have something that behaves a bit like a nervous system. When a leaf is being eaten, a flow of calcium alerts the rest of the plant so it can prepare to defend itself against attack. They have also been shown to alert nearby plants to dangers like drought, disease or insect attacks. The idea of whether plants 'feel pain' is debatable, though.

thought-to-be vegan products?

In 2018, in a video that went viral, BBC comedy panel show *QI* asked which of almonds, avocados, kiwi fruit, melon or butternut squash are suitable for vegans, and their answer was none of them. This is because commercial farming of all of these products, in some parts of the world, involves migratory beekeeping. In some places, there aren't enough local bees and other pollinating insects for the huge orchards, so beehives are transported on the back of trucks between farms. One day they might be on an almond orchard, the next week, they could be moved to an avocado plantation.

So, should the vegans who don't eat honey also be avoiding these commercially farmed fruits and vegetables too? Some might say that the vegans consuming these products are hypocrites, while others might say that this just shows being 100% vegan in modern society is pretty much impossible. One solution might be to avoid anything produced on such a large scale, and instead try to consume only products farmed locally on a far smaller scale. For example, in the UK this method of pollination is not widely used, but things like avocados and almonds imported from places like California may need to be avoided.

It also might depend on your ethical position and moral view about the status of insects, and to what extent they are exploited. Depending on the harvesting methods, the bees may not necessarily be harmed when the honey is gathered or when their hives are transported, but they are more or less slaves. Basically, it all comes down to individual choice and back to the argument that the definition of veganism isn't black and white. Eating an avocado that was commercially farmed might make someone fractionally less vegan compared to someone who abstains, but in the grand scheme of things, does that *really* make a difference?

Are your vegan products eco?

The number of people becoming vegan has increased by more than 150% in the last ten years, with shops and restaurants producing more vegan products than ever, but we should be wondering where all this food is coming from to meet the increased demand. Some take on veganism to tackle damage to the environment caused by

> "Being 100% vegan in modern society is pretty much impossible"

Many vegans avoid products that involve the exploitation of bees

farming and consuming meat, however, are the products in your basket really any better? With lentils coming from Canada, pomegranates and mangoes from India, beans from Brazil, avocados from Mexico, and goji berries from China, are these plant-based diets as environmentally friendly as you think? Surely a lamb chop from the farm down the road is better for the environment than the avocado shipped from the other side of the world? Increased demand for produce like avocados and quinoa has dramatically increased their market price, meaning that they have become too expensive for the people who need them in their country of origin.

It has become obvious that globally we do need to consume less meat and more vegetables, but importing so much from the other side of the

world doesn't seem sensible. Sourcing locally is the best solution. Of course, this approach might limit the range of produce you can get, and will mean some things are a little more expensive, but if your vegan focus is on the environment, then you must understand that importing exotic produce is not an eco solution.

Obviously it's hard to deny that beef and lamb are the most damaging foods for the planet, but it is also tricky to say exactly which diet really is the most environmentally friendly. Vegetables and cereals do have a far smaller carbon footprint compared to meat, but they do still have an impact on ecosystems and biodiversity. There are so many variables to take into consideration, from the origin of the products consumed and farming techniques to the quantity consumed to name a few.

Recently, the soya bean has been widely criticised for its role in the deforestation of South America. Soya is a hugely versatile product that is widely consumed by vegans and vegetarians, and soya beans have become the go-to meat replacement. The US and Brazil produce around

> *"Importing so much from the other side of the world doesn't seem sensible"*

Debatable

Would you eat lab-grown meat? Biologically it is meat, but no animals have to be slaughtered to make it. It creates an ethical loophole, but on the other hand some animals may be exploited for the initial cells to be collected, depending on the production process.

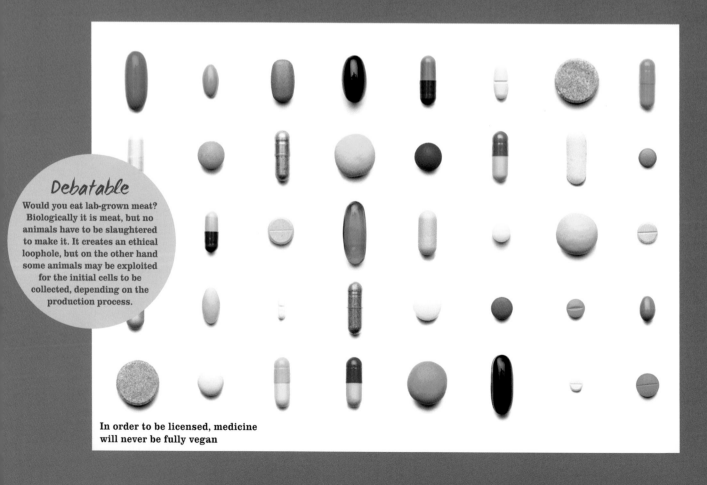

In order to be licensed, medicine will never be fully vegan

Debatable

Should it be okay for vegans to eat eggs from rescued hens? To hens, unfertilised eggs are a waste product, and they produce them whether we eat them or not. If the hens are kept ethically, in a happy, loving home, is it better to eat the eggs than let them go to waste?

If you rescue a hen, should you eat its eggs if they would otherwise go to waste?

The Almeria greenhouses grow vast amounts of produce, but not without a human and environmental cost

64% of the world's supply, and it is Brazil's most lucrative export. However, humans only eat around 6% of the world's supply of soya, with the rest being eaten by livestock, so the responsibility still really lies with the farming of animals.

Is your medicine vegan?

Many medicines contain ingredients or excipients (stabilisers or bulking agents), which aren't suitable for vegans. Plus, in order to gain a product license, medicine has to be tested on non-human animal subjects before human testing, so even if the ingredients are completely vegan they will have been tested on animals. This means that the majority of medicines aren't actually vegan-friendly.

There are some vegan-friendly medicines, although finding them often requires a little research. We certainly wouldn't recommend changing your medication without consulting your doctor, and if there isn't a vegan alternative you might have to make a sacrifice in order to protect your own health. And that is more than okay.

When it comes to medicine and your health,

then consider the Vegan Society's definition of veganism: "Veganism is a way of living which seeks to exclude, *as far as possible and practicable*, all forms of exploitation of, and cruelty to, animals for food, clothing and any other purpose." We make the decision of what is practical in our own lives, and it is down to our own personal decision about what is possible.

How about pets?

We live in a world where keeping a companion animal is the norm, but generally vegans are working towards a society where no animal is kept in captivity. When we buy an animal to be our pet, we're making them our property against their will, and they have absolutely no control over their lives. However, some vegans choose to keep pets that they have rescued from the streets or adopted from sanctuaries, but this still involves keeping them in captivity, so is it really vegan?

Some say that keeping animals in any way is not compatible with the vegan lifestyle, but there are a few varying views. One opinion is that since we live in a society that has domesticated some animals

Did you know

Almeria in Spain is home to Europe's largest greenhouse, covering more than 336 square kilometres (130 square miles). A lot of Europe's fruits and vegetables are grown here (the area produces around 3.5 million tons a year), but many pickers work in 45C (113F) heat for little pay, and live in poor conditions. Plastic and pesticides used also contribute to pollution in the area.

Did you know

Not all supposedly vegan products are cruelty-free – many of us would assume coconut oils and milks are a safe bet, but some coconut farmers in south and southeast Asia use trained monkeys to help harvest their crops, forced to work under gruelling conditions. Get into the habit of researching as much as you can about your products and how they are produced to make sure they are cruelty-free.

then we have a responsibility to continue to take care of them, which means that adopting and rescuing animals in need is okay. Others say that as long as you don't view them as pets, but instead see them as equals then it is acceptable to have them living with you.

Owning service dogs for the disabled is an often-debated subject for many vegans. Veganism is a way of living that looks to exclude all forms of exploitation of animals, where possible. However, for some it might be impossible to survive without a guide dog, for example, so it has to be acceptable to keep them – in these cases the animals aren't pets, they are lifelines. Perhaps as technology develops in the future, there might be more animal-free options to help disabled people in need, which will mean these loyal service animals won't be required.

Humans are animals too

Can you call clothing vegan if human exploitation was involved in its production? Usually when we refer to vegan-friendly clothing, we mean the exclusion of animal products, however, we need to also be questioning who made the clothes too. A single piece of clothing may have affected a number of human lives in its production. Fast fashion should be avoided at all costs – not just by vegans. Fast fashion factories are often sweatshops that are primarily staffed by impoverished women – mainly in Asia – many of whom work for very little pay, in terrible conditions, and have few rights. So even if your new top doesn't contain any animal products, you should probably think about the human cost of its production too.

Human exploitation isn't just an issue when it comes to fast fashion, but the agricultural industry is also guilty. In 2018, a report by the Gangmasters and Labour Abuse Authority exposed the extent of modern-day slavery and exploitation. Between 2016 and 2017 in the UK, an estimated 10,000 and 13,000 people are being exploited in the food and farming industry. There are often stories in the news about horrific conditions, long days and less than minimum wages for fruit pickers in Europe and Australia. Questioning the origin for the produce you are eating should be at the forefront of your mind. Knowing as much

Cruelty-free clothing often focuses on animals, but humans can be exploited for fashion

Although owning a service dog isn't exactly vegan, it is a necessity for some

In a recent interview, Prince Harry cited environmental concerns as a reason why he and Meghan only plan on having two children

Debatable

Is it okay to swat mosquitoes? There are humane traps for pests like rats, but 'cruelty-free' options for insects are rare. The matter is made more complicated by insects that spread diseases (like mosquitoes and ticks). It's often down to where individuals draw their own ethical lines.

"An effective way people can reduce their carbon emissions is to have fewer children"

as you can about the produce that you eat will ensure you can rest easy that no living thing was exploited in its production.

Do you need to have fewer children to be vegan?

This probably comes down to your own definition of veganism. Many believe that people should limit the number of children they have for the environment. In a recent *Vogue* interview, Prince Harry said that: "I've always thought: this place is borrowed," after stating that he only plans to have two children, "And, surely, being as intelligent as we all are, or as evolved as we all are supposed to be, we should be able to leave something better behind for the next generation."

A study in 2017 published in *Environmental*

Research Letters cited that the most effective way that people can reduce their carbon emissions is to have fewer children. The researchers estimated that having one fewer child would save an individual 58.6 tons of CO_2-equivalent per year of their life. Although overpopulation is a controversial topic in the climate-change debate, it can't be ignored. Having children isn't an obviously vegan issue, but for anyone concerned about the environment and every individual's impact upon it, this can be a very real decision to consider.

in short: It's complicated

It shouldn't be assumed that veganism is an all-or-nothing way of life. Instead of quantifying the 'level' of vegan someone is, or scrutinising every grey area in the neverending quest for the most ethical way of life, we should instead focus on the positive impacts of being vegan. Being truly 100% vegan is pretty much impossible – we should concentrate on what is important and realistic for us as individuals, without judging the lifestyle choices of others.

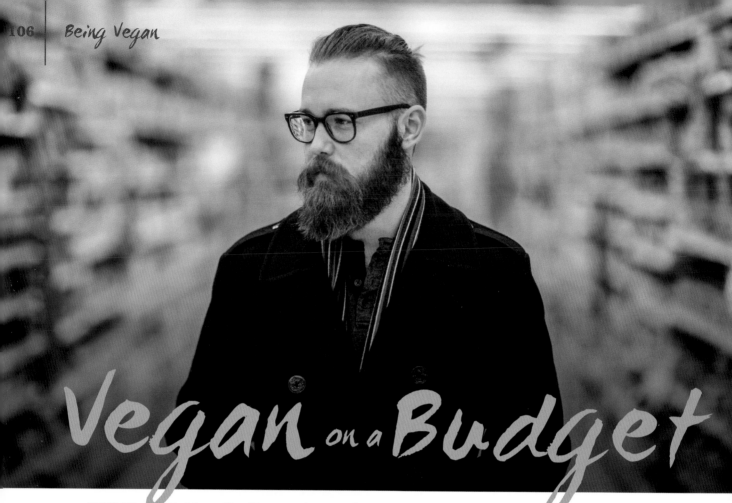

Vegan on a Budget

With a bit of planning & creativity, a vegan diet is possible no matter your budget

One of the main misconceptions of a vegan lifestyle is that it's expensive. If you live on branded meat substitutes, ready meals and supplements then yes, it can become pretty costly, but there are ways to create healthy and filling vegan meals without emptying your bank account.

Cook at home

Vegan or not, eating out comes with a cost. The more you can cook from scratch at home the more money you'll save. The base ingredients of most vegan favourites are grains, pulses and vegetables, all of which can be bought cheaply. Buy loose goods when you can, as you often end up paying more when a product is packaged.

Build up a repertoire of meals you can cook quickly with the staples you always keep in the cupboards. There are plenty of websites that will suggest recipes based on the ingredients you have available – particularly useful when it's nearly time for the weekly shop and you want to use up what you have left.

Limit specialist vegan foods

It's an exciting time to be vegan, with new vegan-friendly products appearing on the shelves all the time, but these specialist items often come with a hefty price tag. These foods are best seen as occasional treats if you're on a tight budget. Be especially aware of products dressed up in fancy packaging with 'vegan' all over it when the food inside is something that's usually suitable for vegans anyway; do you really need to buy the expensive vegan spread when the own-brand sunflower spread is a fraction of the price? Cheaper versions of foods like pastries and sweet pies are often incidentally vegan-friendly because they contain margarine or vegetable oil instead of butter.

Shop wisely

Making a shopping list and sticking to it is one of the best things you can do for your wallet. Plan the week's meals ahead or just list the staples you know you're running low on, then head to the shops and buy only what you've written down (unless you find something reduced to a few pence). If you can't be trusted around pretty displays and tempting offers, set yourself a strict time limit so you have to go directly to the things you need and don't get distracted.

Get to know your local shops. Find out the time they tend to reduce items, work out where they put their best offers, and apply for a loyalty card so you can start building up points. Be aware that supermarkets want you to notice their new products and the offers that only save you a bit of money, so these are displayed at eye-level or on the ends of aisles. Look at the very bottom shelf; this is

"Specialist vegan-friendly products often come with a hefty price tag"

where they'll usually tuck the real bargains.

If you want to find new ingredients and meal options, go to the shops on a recce but don't buy anything. Make a note of the price of each item, then compare it to other stores and search online to find out which recipes you can use it in. Try venturing outside of your usual supermarkets; you'll often find foods like noodles, tofu and coconut milk for a lower price at Asian stores, and health shops and online stores will sometimes have great offers.

Minimise waste

Getting organised is the first step to reducing the amount of food you throw away – if you stick to your list or meal plan you won't end up buying things you don't need or won't use before they go off. It's inevitable, though, that there will be times you end up with a lone carrot nearing the end of its life or a third of a can of tomatoes. Don't throw

A bag of frozen veg saves time, money and waste

Store cupboard STAPLES

- Chickpeas
- Lentils
- Brown rice
- Potatoes
- Sweet potatoes
- Egg-free pasta
- Oats
- Tinned tomatoes
- Vegetable oil
- Onions
- Garlic
- Frozen peas
- Frozen fruit
- Popcorn
- Nuts & seeds
- Tofu
- Coconut milk
- Dark chocolate
- Vegetable stock
- Herbs and spices

Sometimes nature provides food that costs nothing at all

A network of thrifty vegan friends can prove invaluable

this food away. Instead, get creative and find ways to use it up. Soup is a great option; quick and easy to make, it works with all sorts of ingredients. Invest in a hand blender (you can find them for as little as £10/$15) and you'll be able to whizz together any leftover vegetables and pulses with some vegetable stock to create a filling meal.

If you have ingredients left that really won't work in a soup, find out whether you can freeze, dry or pickle them. There are numerous guides online that will help you save fruits, vegetables and herbs for another day.

Go for frozen

Fresh fruits and vegetables can be expensive, especially if you're buying them out of season, and they can go to waste if you don't use them in time. Consider buying frozen instead and just defrosting the amount you need for a recipe. Frozen fruit and veg are often much cheaper than their fresh counterparts, and they're no less tasty or nutritious; everything is picked at its peak and

frozen within hours, so you're not losing out on any goodness.

Batch cook

If you have room in your freezer after packing away all your leftovers and frozen vegetables, it's worth getting into the habit of batch cooking. When you're making something like a curry or a chilli for dinner, make more than you need for that night – especially if the recipe calls for half a tin of this or half a pack of that and you can save waste by doubling up on everything. Seal the leftover portions in airtight containers once everything has cooled down, then store them in the freezer. Next time you're home late, running behind schedule or just not in the mood to cook you can defrost and reheat your home cooking rather than reaching for a pricey ready meal or ordering a takeaway.

Think outside the shops

If you have a patio, a balcony, or even a windowsill

you can grow your own food. Fresh herbs are expensive and don't last very long, so investing in a few plants and pinching off leaves when you need them will save you money in the long run. With a garden or access to an allotment comes even more opportunity – find out which fruits and vegetables grow well in your climate and soon you'll be experiencing the pride of eating something you produced yourself.

Sometimes you don't even need to get your watering can out because nature does the work for you. When fruits like blackberries are in season, head out to the hedgerows with a bag full of containers and stock up on free fruit. Add berries to your breakfast, bake with them or freeze them to keep your sweet tooth satisfied during the rest of the year. If you live near the coast you could try foraging for seaweed – just make sure you know which kinds are edible, and check local regulations about what you can and can't take from the shore.

Get a little help from your friends

If you have friends or relatives who have been vegan longer than you, or are known to be great with a budget, make use of their expertise. Ask for a list of their go-to staple ingredients, find out where they go for great bargains and how they make sure nothing goes to waste. Swap recipes and tips – you might both each learn something valuable from each other.

If you know a number of other vegans, invite everyone round for a potluck. Each person contributes one dish or a couple of sides and it quickly turns into a feast. You'll get a huge variety of food and you might find your new favourite budget recipe. If anything is left over at the end of the night, you'll all have lunch sorted for the next day.

> "Don't throw leftover food away – get creative and find ways to use it up"

Top money-saving tips

1 EAT BEFORE YOU SHOP
Shop hungry and you're much more likely to stray from your list and make impulsive choices.

2 PACK A LUNCH
Finding vegan food out and about can get expensive, so take the time to prepare lunch before you leave the house.

3 SHOP AROUND
Prices can vary hugely between stores so make a note of the cheapest place to buy each of your staples.

4 GO BIG
For foods you eat regularly, buying bigger packets often works out cheaper per gram or ounce overall.

5 MAKE YOUR OWN DIPS
Pre-made dips like hummus and salsa can be pricey, but they're easy to recreate at home.

Many vegan meals can be made using ingredients you already have in your kitchen

The Power of Plant Protein

Meeting our protein requirements with plant-based foods, rather than animal-based foods, can both improve health and help solve the climate crisis

The importance of protein

When it comes to a plant-based, vegan diet there is one question that pops up particularly frequently: "But how would I get enough protein?" Ensuring a sufficient protein intake is undoubtedly important, as our bodies need protein to function: every single cell of the body contains protein, with the majority present in our muscles. How much protein do we need in our diets to remain healthy? The general rule of thumb is a daily minimum of 0.8 grams of protein for every kilogram of your body weight – though if the protein is fully from plant-based sources, the recommended daily intake increases to 0.9g of protein per kilogram of body weight, as plant proteins are typically harder to digest. But a balanced vegan diet that incorporates a wide range of plant protein sources can easily meet our bodies' requirements for protein – while also providing significant positive impacts, particularly on our health and our environmental footprints, the latter of which are currently far overshooting planetary boundaries.

Plant-based for health

For optimal health, it's not the case of the more protein, the better. In the words of Harvard School of Public Health: "It's all about the protein 'package'". A study of 130,000 men and women found that the percentage of calories from protein intake did not have an impact on mortality or disease, but – perhaps unsurprisingly – the *source* of that protein did matter.

Even the most protein rich-foods also contain other ingredients, like saturated or unsaturated fats, fiber and sodium. When looking at the complete package of protein-rich foods, plant protein is typically superior to animal protein: a steak may offer a lot of protein, but it also comes with the unwanted side effects of too much saturated fat. Lentils, on the other hand, offer less protein, but the protein that's there is complemented by significant amounts of fiber (which most of us don't get enough of).

When plant-based protein sources do include fats, they are typically unsaturated fats, which help to lower cholesterol – another positive.

As a result of superior 'protein packaging' in plant-based foods, relying on plants rather than animals to

"Considering the complete food 'package' plant protein is typically superior to animal protein"

meet our essential protein needs is linked to a whole host of positive health benefits: lower risk of cardiovascular disease, type 2 diabetes, cancer, obesity and being overweight. While some of the studies base these positive health findings on vegetarian diets – which means some protein intake still comes from dairy products – vegetarians typically have a high share of plant protein in their diets, as they eat more whole grains, legumes, nuts, seeds and vegetables than non-vegetarians. Whether fully plant-based or not, excluding processed meat and red meat as sources of protein is undoubtedly advisable: the World Health Organization has called out processed meat as a cause for cancer and stated that red meat is "probably carcinogenic" too. Despite these health benefits, a recent study found evidence of one drawback of mainly plant-based diets, linking vegetarian and vegan diets to a higher risk of stroke – though the reasons for this are not yet clear.

Plant-based for the climate

Beyond overall positive health impacts, shifting to plant-based sources of protein could have a hugely positive environmental effect. The animal products with the lowest environmental impact still exceeds plant-based sources of protein. The environmental effects would be largest in developed economies, where the intake of animal foods is currently the highest. A 2018 study published in well-renowned health journal *The Lancet* found that in high-income countries, replacing animal-sourced foods with plant-based ones could reduce greenhouse gas emissions by up to 84%. Read more about the potential impacts of global veganism on page 9.

The flexitarian option

For many, going fully plant-based may be too drastic a change, but even a partial shift to plant-based proteins would have huge benefits. If everyone globally adopted a plant-based flexitarian diet – one that is plant-based two-thirds of the time, but allow from a small intake of animal protein – we could reduce greenhouse gas emissions by as much as 52% by 2050, while also reaping health-benefits. So, get your protein from plants when possible – whether completely or partially.

Proteins are essential for healthy functioning bodies, particularly muscles

A varied plant-based diet can meet protein requirements

Top plant protein sources

The total daily recommended intake of protein matters, but it's not all about the total amount: eating a wide variety of plant-based foods is necessary to get all the nine essential amino acids, the building blocks of proteins that the body can't make on its own.

How much protein is found per 100 calories of these vegan-friendly sources?

- Tofu: **10.7g**
- Lentils, cooked: **7.8g**
- Beans, including black-eyed, pinto, and kidney: between **6.3-6.7g**
- Broccoli: **6.7g**
- Chickpeas, cooked: **5.4g**
- Whole wheat bread: **5.4g**
- Nuts and seeds: e.g. almonds **3.7g**
- Quinoa*, cooked: **3.4g**

*quinoa is a complete protein which means it contains all 22 amino acids

The Vegan Home

From candles to cushions, and polish to paint, curating a vegan home is easier than ever

Developed as a sustainable alternative to leather, Piñatex is made from pineapple-leaf fibre

For most, veganism goes far beyond diet; it's a way of life. And, while food is often the first step, making the rest of your home vegan-friendly can be much trickier to navigate. Before transitioning from an everyday household to a vegan one, there are a number of items that need to be purged from your nest. While most are pretty obvious, some are downright surprising. And, the fact that there's no single vegan standard for homeware can muddy the already murky waters.

A soft touch

Although leather armchairs and suede sofas are a no-go, vegan alternatives abound. In addition to the common options like polyurethane, more innovative solutions are beginning to make their mark, such as Piñatex, a PETA-approved leather alternative made from pineapple-leaf fibre; and Apple Ten Lork, which is created using discarded apple skins.

Meanwhile, finding alternatives to feather or down cushions and mattresses has never been easier. Some vegan options are made from natural ingredients like buckwheat or coconut husks, others from gel fibre or memory foam. The Linen Cupboard's Smartdown Vegan Eco Pillows are even crafted from recycled plastic bottles and sustainably sourced cotton.

Cotton also makes a brilliant earth-friendly, non-synthetic alternative to wool blankets, particularly those made from organic cotton, which is grown with fewer pesticides. Brands such as West Elm and Kantha Quilts offer an array of options as friendly on the eyes as they are on the environment.

DIY all-purpose cleaning spray

- 500 ml | 17 fl oz warm, purified water
- 50 ml | 1¾ fl oz castile soap
- 5 drops each of: lemon oil, orange oil, tea tree oil and eucalyptus oil
- 240 ml | 8 fl oz | 1 cup apple cider vinegar
- 1 tbsp baking soda

METHOD

- Pour the warm water into a large, clean spray bottle.
- Add the remaining ingredients and shake well to combine.
- Use immediately.

Get the glow

Whether you prefer scented, hand-poured or organic, candles often contain animal-derived ingredients like stearic acid and beeswax. However, some home fragrance brands – such as Octō, Evil Queen, Paddywax and Hobo – are embracing animal-free ingredients like soy, coconut and vegetable wax.

Paint it green

When you're halfway up a ladder, it's easy to forget that even though wall paints are labelled eco-friendly, most not only contain animal products, but are tested on animals too. Nasty ingredients to look out for include casein, shellac and ox gall. Luckily, popular brands such as Lakeland Paints, Sherwin Williams and Auro offer vegan ranges, free from toxic ingredients and odours.

A clean sweep

Being vegan also extends into the cupboard beneath the sink. While many steer clear of chemical-laden cleaning products, traditional offerings can contain up to ten animal-derived ingredients. Instead of the beeswax often used in natural furniture polishes, vegan varieties feature olive or orange oil. When in doubt, search for the Leaping Bunny logo – the only internationally recognised symbol that certifies that no new animal tests were used in product development. Alternatively, look for labels that state 'free from anima l ingredients' or 'entirely plant-based'.

Paint often includes animal-derived ingredients like casein, shellac and ox gall

Laundry day

Although we all want our laundry to come out of the dryer feeling cloud-like, many fabric softeners contain animal ingredients, including tallow or lanolin, and most detergents are tested on animals too. Fortunately, Ecover, Mrs. Meyer's, Method, Seventh Generation and Dr. Bronner's all offer vegan laundry solutions. And, for the earth-conscious, the ingenious Ecoegg is even reusable.

Screen time

While it's relatively easy to source vegan alternatives for most items, others can be much trickier to track down. Surprisingly, LCD screens, including televisions, computers, phones and tablets, all contain animal cholesterol. Unfortunately, there aren't currently any vegan substitutes on the market.

"televisions, computers, phones and tablets contain animal cholesterol"

From buckwheat to memory foam, there are a number of substitutes for feather and down pillows

It can be a challenge to incorporate veganism into your health, beauty and haircare regime – but we're here to help clear things up!

You've cut out all meat, fish, dairy and other animal products from your diet. You've donated all your leather jackets and wool jumpers to charity. But one thing's just not right yet – your beauty collection. With all the mystery surrounding animal testing, and jargon terms hiding what ingredients aren't actually vegan, it's hard to know how to veganise your dressing table. But by the time you've finished reading this article, you'll know exactly what to look for when you buy new cosmetics, and learn how to swap your shampoo for vegan-friendly alternatives.

Vegan beauty, in a nutshell, is any skincare, haircare, or cosmetic product that contains zero animal products. All the ingredients must be plant-based, or synthetic without the involvement of animals. This ensures you are not inadvertently supporting factory farming, or the use/slaughter of animals, by using products that have been made with animal-based ingredients. With so much choice available to you, every purchase you make tells retailers and manufacturers what customers are looking for. As more and more people choose vegan products instead of animal-based ones, we are sending a powerful message to big companies – that we will no longer tolerate animal use in any form.

Is it cruelty-free?

But vegan cosmetics aren't simply products with no animal usage. Vegans should also be looking to buy completely cruelty-free products, which means that at no part of the manufacturing process is the product (or its ingredients) tested on animals.

Vegan Health and Beauty

Cosmetic testing on animals was outlawed in the EU in 2009, in the UK in 1998, and in India in 2014. The good news is that many other countries around the world are looking to introduce similar laws. The bad news, however, is that the industry still has a long way to go – China, one of the biggest markets for cosmetic goods, requires that products sold in its territories are tested on animals. This means that non-Chinese companies have to test on animals if they want to sell in China, including some of the biggest companies – Maybelline, L'Oréal, MaxFactor and more still partake in animal testing. Companies do tend to put profit before animal welfare.

The fact that so many big companies do test on animals muddies the water even further. Some brands might claim to be completely cruelty-free and vegan, but if the brand is owned by a larger company that does test on animals, buying those brands indirectly supports animal testing. Up until 2017, that stalwart of cruelty-free, animal welfare conscious beauty The Body Shop was actually owned by L'Oreal, meaning that if you purchased a Body Shop product, you were handing money to a company that partook in animal testing. However, the Body Shop was recently purchased by Brazilian company Natura, which has been completely cruelty-free since 2009. So, if you are looking to

Non-vegan ingredients

Demystifying the many curious chemicals and compounds found in beauty products

When you buy food, you generally know what's vegan and what's not at a glance. If a product has any meat, dairy, eggs or fish-based ingredient, you'll put it down straight away. But since cosmetics are manufactured with all sorts of chemicals and non-edible ingredients, it can be difficult to understand what the label is actually telling you. So, we'll sum up the most common, non-vegan cosmetic ingredients to look out for:

- *Lanolin* is derived from sheep's wool, and is commonly used in moisturising products.
- *Gelatin* is a by-product of animal slaughter, and should always be avoided by vegans.
- *Beeswax* is produced by honey bees, and is used as an emulsion.
- *Collagen* is made by boiling animal components, and you'll find it in many anti-ageing products.
- *Glycerin* is found in both animal and plant fats, so if a product has glycerin in it, look for a 'Vegan' logo on the packaging.
- *Keratin* comes from animal horns, nails and hair, and is often used in shampoo and conditioners.
- *Cochineal* is a red pigment that comes from crushed beetles, so look out for this in lipstick.
- *Squalene* originates in the livers of sharks, and is often used in moisturisers and foundations.
- *Guanine* is derived from fish scales, and is used to add a shimmer effect to powders.
- *Silk powder* isn't vegan as it's spun by insects, but you'll find it in many makeup and skincare products.

Make your own body scrub

Gently exfoliate your skin with this quick and easy recipe, courtesy of Amy Wheller @amymaysews

INGREDIENTS

- 225g | 8oz granulated sugar (the bigger grains, the better)
- 110g | 4oz coconut oil
- ½ tbsp olive oil
- 10 drops of your favourite essential oil (such as lavender, tea tree, rose)

METHOD

1. Melt the coconut oil over a low heat, and remove from the heat as soon as it becomes liquid.
2. Add the olive oil so the coconut oil remains in its liquid state permanently. Set the oil aside to cool down.
3. Stir in the essential oil.
4. Add in a bit of the sugar at a time, and mix slowly. Keep adding and mixing until the scrub reaches the consistency you want.
5. Store in a sterilised, airtight container like a clean glass jar.

Around 80% of Lush's products are vegan. The company offer packaging-free products too, to help cut down on waste

Vegan-friendly brands

Lush
uk.lush.com

Arguably the most famous cruelty-free brand out there, all of Lush's products are vegetarian, and most of them are also vegan, plus they smell fantastic. Many items are plastic- or packaging-free, too.

Body Shop
thebodyshop.com

The Body Shop's entire range is completely vegetarian and cruelty-free, and their vegan products (made without honey, beeswax etc) are clearly labelled. Their packaging can be recycled in stores, too.

E.L.F
elfcosmetics.co.uk

This makeup and skincare brand is great for the money-saving vegan, as it's affordable, cruelty-free, and comes highly recommended by YouTube makeup artists.

Charlotte Tilbury
charlottetilbury.com

This high-end beauty brand from makeup artist Charlotte Tilbury has a glamorous retro vibe is totally cruelty-free. The website helpfully labels which of the brand's products are vegan.

Anastasia Beverly Hills
anastasiabeverlyhills.co.uk

This professional makeup brand is the go-to for makeup artists, especially their eyeshadow range. All its products are cruelty-free, but you'll need to check the website to see which ones are vegan.

Arbonne
arbonne.com

All of Arbonne's lovely skincare and makeup products are vegan and cruelty-free. Better still, they're all based on botanicals, so they feel more natural on the skin.

purchase from a brand, it's wise to check if it has a parent company, and whether that company tests on animals.

Shop smart

By this point, you might be thinking that it's very difficult to find products that are both vegan and cruelty-free. However, fear not – you'll be surprised at just how easy it is. Just head to your local shopping centre, and see what you can find. Many cruelty-free brands clearly mark which products are suitable for vegans on their packaging, so just pick up a product and look for a 'suitable for vegans' label. If you're in the UK, Superdrug is the best place to start, as all of their own-brand beauty, skincare and haircare products are actually vegan.

To make it even easier to spot vegan buys, you can look for certain logos. For cruelty-free certified products, you're either looking for the Leaping Bunny (a bunny surrounded by stars), the Caring Consumer (a bunny with pink love heart ears), or the CCF logo (a silhouette of a bunny). Vegan products are a bit easier to spot – just look for a big green 'V' or the word 'Vegan' anywhere on the product's packaging.

Now you understand exactly what products you are looking for, you can be much more selective when it comes to purchasing health and beauty products. The power is in your hands – you can put your money where your mouth is, and tell the big companies that animal usage is wrong.

> "Many brands clearly mark which products are suitable for vegans on their packaging"

Watch out for certain ingredients, as they may not be vegan

Vitamins, minerals & supplements

Don't just look after yourself on the outside – avoid the pitfalls of poor nutrition and boost your health from the inside out

When you say you're going vegan, you will often face questions about where you'll get your nutrients from. It's commonly believed that vegans lack protein, calcium, iron, omega-3 and vitamin B12 – but if you do your research on what you eat, you can easily replace the vitamins found in dairy, meat and eggs with nutrient-rich vegan sources. It's best to get your vitamins and minerals from your food as much as possible, but – in addition to carefully managing your diet – you can take supplements to boost your nutrients if there are any you regularly miss out on. Be careful, though, as some of these products contain gelatin, which is a big no-no. Check the label before buying, as many supermarkets, pharmacists and health food stores do sell vegan-friendly supplements.

Calcium

Non-vegan sources
MILK, CHEESE, YOGHURT

Vegan-friendly sources
SOYA PRODUCTS, GREEN VEG

Calcium is necessary for strong bones and teeth, so you need enough of it to stop your bones from becoming brittle. It's easy enough to access, so consume plenty of vegan dairy replacements!

Iron

Non-vegan sources
RED MEAT, CHICKEN

Vegan-friendly sources
PULSES, FORTIFIED CEREALS, WHOLEGRAIN BREAD

You need iron for your red blood cells, and deficiency can cause severe problems like anaemia. Top up your supplies by eating lots of wholegrains, beans and pulses.

Vitamin B12

Non-vegan sources
RED MEAT, FISH, EGGS

Vegan-friendly sources
YEAST PRODUCTS, FORTIFIED NON-DAIRY MILKS, CEREALS

B12 is one of those nutrients few of us get enough of, regardless of our diet. However, we need it for healthy blood and a healthy nervous system.

Vitamin D

Non-vegan sources
FISH, CHEESE, EGG YOLKS

Vegan-friendly sources
SUNLIGHT, FORTIFIED FATTY SPREADS, SUPPLEMENTS

Vitamin D is what the sun gives us, and helps to keep our bones, teeth and muscles healthy. You can get it from foods, too, but the best source is a regular dose of sunshine.

Omega-3

Non-vegan sources
OILY FISH

Vegan-friendly sources
LINSEED, RAPESEED, WALNUTS, SOY PRODUCTS

Omega-3 lowers our risk of heart disease, and helps maintain good heart health. Research suggests vegan sources may not be as effective as oily fish, though.

Zinc

Non-vegan sources
MEAT, SHELLFISH

Vegan-friendly sources
LEGUMES, NUTS AND SEEDS

Zinc is required by over 300 enzymes in your body, so it's crucial to eat about 10mg of it per day. This can be done as part of a balanced diet.

Choline

Non-vegan sources
EGGS, MILK, BEEF

Vegan-friendly sources
QUINOA, CRUCIFEROUS VEG, MUSHROOMS

Choline is essential for healthy metabolism, nerves and brain function. It's not a particularly well-known nutrient so is easy to overlook. Adults should aim for 425-550mg per day.

Fashion
with a
Conscience

Gone are the days when vegan fashion meant compromise, today your wardrobe can look good, and do good too

With iconic brands like Givenchy, Lanvin and Saint Laurent embracing vegan 'leather', and the inaugural Vegan Fashion Week, there's never been a better time to curate a cruelty-free wardrobe. And, while veganism is certainly en vogue, overhauling your entire closet is no mean feat; it takes time, commitment and resources. Think of it as a slow and steady transition, not a weekend shopping spree, because realistically, it will take between six months and a year to veganise your wardrobe.

Evaluate your closet

First thing's first, determine what items in your wardrobe are already vegan. Silk, wool, down, shearling, mohair and cashmere are serious faux pas, as are the usual suspects; leather, suede, exotic skins, feathers and fur. On the other hand, anything that's 100% cotton is a good starting point, so t-shirts, jeans and summer dresses are generally a safe bet.

However, hold off on the bonfire – what to do with non-vegan items is a personal choice. While some opt to slowly phase them out, using them until they need to be replaced, others choose to donate or sell them. Whatever your preference, just don't throw them in the bin and contribute to the growing landfill crisis. According to experts, by 2050, fashion is on course to use up more than a quarter of the world's carbon budget.

In the know

From cotton to polyurethane (PU) and hemp to linen, animal-free fashion has never been cooler, or more varied. Keep an eye out for items made from cork, bamboo and canvas, along with other innovative, eco-friendly fabrics like seed, mushroom and pineapple fibre.

Another wonderful cruelty-free alternative is Tencel (or lyocell), a semi-natural material cleverly crafted from plants. For knits, modal and micromodal work just as well as wool, and satin blends emulate silk to smooth perfection. Other options, such as fabrics made from cellulose fibres, are also being developed.

Although synthetics like nylon, polyester and acrylic are vegan, recycled versions are gentler on the planet. Meanwhile, hi-tech fabrics are proving more sustainable than ever before, such as econyl, which is regenerated from discarded fishing nets and carpets.

When it comes to vegan leather alternatives, not all are created equal. Fake 'leather' gets a bad rap for looking cheap, shiny and brittle, but matte pieces with a little grain transcend the much-decried 'pleather' look. Today, most vegan 'leather' is made of PU, but this may soon make way for cutting-edge bio-fabricated substitutes, grown in labs.

Be mindful

With vegan fashion is on the rise, so too is mindful consumerism. Shoppers should remember that just because a piece of clothing is made from vegan components, doesn't mean it's sustainable. It's always important to ask about the manufacturing process, materials, labour practices and carbon footprint. When it comes to fast fashion brands, they may offer on-trend, well-designed pieces, but they're often poorly made and ethically dubious.

Ultimately, the goal is to build a wardrobe filled with high-quality, long-lasting and timeless pieces that will carry you from season to season and help you consume at a much slower pace – it's about curating, not collecting. In addition, vintage or second-hand shopping is a practical and sustainable way to replenish your wardrobe, while keeping items out of landfills.

Animal-friendly fashion

Stella McCartney
stellamccartney.com
The queen of cruelty-free fashion, Stella McCartney's faux leather jackets have been a vegan staple for decades.

Beyond Skin
beyond-skin.com
From on-trend mules to classic Mary Janes, Beyond Skin's trademark vintage-inspired shoes are not only vegan and sustainable, but they're handcrafted in Spain.

Matt & Nat
mattandnat.com
This brand makes affordable and attractive bags, using vegan leather and lining crafted from recycled plastic bottles.

Dr. Martens
drmartens.com
The iconic shoe brand offers a range of vegan boots and sandals, complete with Dr. Martens' signature yellow stitching.

Fjordson
fjordson.com
Not only does this Swiss watch brand use vegan leather, it donates 5% of revenue to an animal shelter, boasts carbon-neutral shipping and uses recycled materials in its packaging.

Nanushka
nanushka.com
While Nanushka's vegan puffer jacket has reached cult status, the company offers a wide variety of other faux leather pieces including skirts, dresses and coats.

Faux leather, not faux sustainability

Although vegan alternatives to leather can mitigate your carbon footprint, some are even more damaging than by-products of animal slaughter

At best, leather is a by-product of the meat industry and, at worst, an industry unto itself. But beware, just because a vegan material is good for the animals, doesn't mean it's automatically better for the planet.

Most vegan faux leathers are made of PU or PVC. These are non-biodegradable plastics, made from fossil fuels, whose properties can quite easily mimic those of leather. Thanks to its low production cost, PVC, is one of the world's most popular plastics. However, it is also among the most toxic

pollutants in the world, and the single most damaging plastic, according to Greenpeace.

PVC is not only made from carcinogenic chemicals, but produces huge amounts of waste that pollute land, air and sea alike – pollution that disproportionately affects low-income populations. For a more sustainable solution, seek out cork, canvas and pineapple fabrics, or even recycled synthetics, rather than plastics.

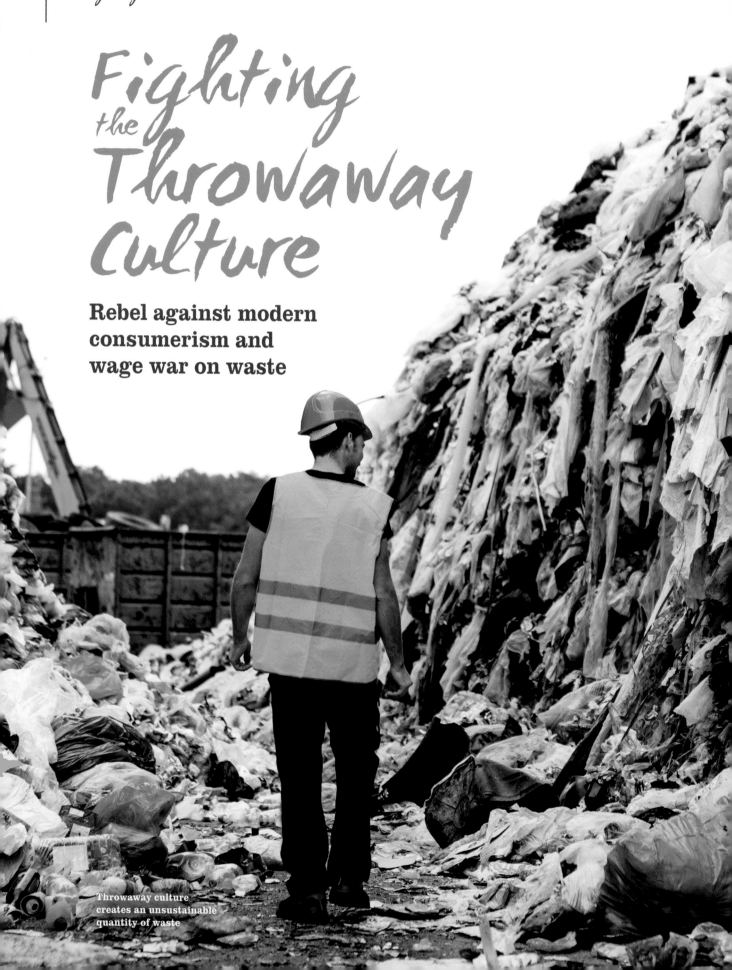

Fighting the Throwaway Culture

Rebel against modern consumerism and wage war on waste

Throwaway culture
creates an unsustainable
quantity of waste

For many people, the aim of veganism is to minimise cruelty to and exploitation of animals. While diet plays a large part in this, it's often a lifestyle choice that extends beyond the kitchen. Waste and consumerism have huge impacts on wildlife and the environment, creating pollution and damaging habitats.

Between 1905 and 2005, New York City saw a tenfold increase in the amount of packaging and discarded products per person collected as waste. The UK generated almost 223 million tons of waste in 2016. 104 million tons were recycled or 'otherwise recovered', but almost a quarter ended up in landfill. Countries like America and the UK offload vast quantities of their waste onto developing countries because exporting it is cheaper and easier than trying to process it all within the country. Previously, much of the UK's waste was shipped to China, but since China imposed a ban on the import of plastics, an increasing amount has been sent to other countries including Malaysia, Thailand, and Vietnam. The waste is sent to be recycled or otherwise safely disposed of, but there have been reports of waste management companies dealing with the materials inadequately and allowing them to end up in rivers and oceans.

One of the reasons we're more wasteful than ever is planned obsolescence. When mass production took off in the 1920s and 1930s manufacturers realised that the longer a product lasted the less need a customer would have to purchase a replacement, so they began to design products and parts that would stop working after a few years. Added to ever-changing trends and the power of advertising to make consumers believe they need the newest version of everything, planned obsolescence ensures that we're frequently replacing items that would once have lasted decades. Recycling can reduce the effects of this alarming business strategy, but it is not always the answer.

As well-known as it is, the recycling icon is often misunderstood. If the icon appears on a product it means it can be recycled, but it doesn't necessarily mean your local council or recycling centre will accept it. Each facility has its own policy, so familiarise yourself with what can and can't go in your recycling bin and try not to buy items that will be rejected. Recycling kitchen waste is becoming the norm in many households, but don't forget about the rest of the house; put two small bins in your bathroom, bedroom and living room to remind yourself that all your household waste should be sorted and properly disposed of.

Recycling helps minimise the amount of waste that goes to landfill, but it's the last of the '3 Rs' – reduce, reuse and recycle. Recycling is a complicated process and still uses energy and resources, so reducing and reusing should always be your first options. In a world that's always telling people they need to buy more and have the newest things to be happy, here are some ways to combat throwaway culture. Although it may not feel like it, your choices as an individual affect the decisions made by policy makers and large corporations. Make a few changes in your shopping and lifestyle habits and you can change the world.

Food and drink

Vegan cooking relies on a lot of vegetables, pulses and nuts, most of which are sold in unnecessary amount of packaging in supermarkets. Take your own cotton bags to the shops and buy loose items wherever possible. Find out whether there's a zero-

Bring bags and jars to the shops to avoid unnecessary packaging

waste shop nearby – these stores allow customers to take their own containers and fill them with foods ranging from beans and cereals to apple cider vinegar and nut butter. Make sure you're realistic about the food you need to buy; think through your meals for the week ahead and try to buy only what you need. Find out how best to store each item so you're not left with stale bread and wilted leaves. Beeswax wraps keep products fresh and just need to be washed in cold water, so you don't have to rely on clingfilm or foil to seal leftovers and lunches.

Disposable tableware grew in popularity with the rise of fast food restaurants; cheap and easy to make, it cut down on cleaning and meant customers could clear their own tables. Now plastic cutlery is a major contributor to the vast amounts of avoidable waste produced each year. The easiest way to combat this problem is to carry your own set of cutlery – sets are made from metal, bamboo, recycled plastic and other more sustainable materials, and by keeping cutlery in your bag you'll never be caught short when you decide to eat out.

In the UK alone, more than 35 million plastic bottles are thrown away every year. In a country where tap water is readily available and completely safe, there's no need for this many single-use bottles. Carry a reusable bottle with you – not only does it cut down on waste, a good quality bottle will save you money and keep your water cool on hot days. More and more refill stations are appearing in buildings and public spaces, and the Refill app will help you locate the nearest place to top up. But water bottles aren't the only problem. Disposable coffee cups might look like they're made from paper but they're often lined with plastic to stop them going soggy. An estimated 7 million disposable cups are used every single day in the UK, and because they're plastic-lined and contaminated with drink, very few are recycled. Invest in a reusable flask or cup and ask baristas to use it for your hot drink instead – this cuts down on waste and often keeps your drink hot for longer. Some companies even offer discounts to customers who bring their own cups.

Cosmetics & toiletries

An estimated 120 billion items of packaging from the cosmetics industry are thrown away each year along with products like cotton buds, face wipes and nappies. Most of it goes to landfill or ends up being shipped to other countries for

Policies for the planet

On the 5th October 2015 England followed the example of the rest of the UK and introduced a charge for single-use plastic bags at large retailers. The charge was brought in to minimise the number thrown away by encouraging shoppers to bring reusable bags with them. Since its introduction it's estimated that the charge has led to an 86 per cent reduction in the number of single-use bags given out by retailers, preventing billions of plastic bags ending up in landfill or littering the landscape. The average English person now uses 19 bags per year, compared with 140 before the charge.

Menstrual cups hold much more blood than tampons and need to be changed less often

> "In the UK alone, more than 35 million plastic bottles are thrown away every year"

Electronic devices are often designed to fail after a few years

disposal. Where possible, choose biodegradable cotton buds and wipes or buy reusable versions instead. It's often hard to avoid packaging when buying cosmetics and toiletries, but an increasing number of companies are beginning to sell 'naked' products and refills. Other manufactures have launched recycling schemes – return a certain amount of empty packaging and you'll receive a voucher or free product. Making the effort to bring your own containers, top up a product you've used up or return an empty container cuts down on your household waste and sends a message to the cosmetics industry that there is a demand for sustainable beauty.

90 per cent of all sanitary products contain plastic, and over 1 billion items are thrown away every year. Tampons also get flushed down the toilet, eventually ending up on beaches or in the sea. Looked after properly, reusable menstrual cups can last for 10 years. This could prevent hundreds of tampons from being thrown away, and making the swap can save a lot of money. They can be an intimidating concept, but many people report greater comfort and less cramping with cups than with tampons. If a menstrual cup isn't an option, consider reusable sanitary pads. These soft cotton pads can be bought or made at home, and simply go in the wash once they've been used. Plastic applicators are the longest-lasting part of a tampon, so try to use non-applicator or cardboard applicator varieties if you decide to continue using tampons. And whichever products you use, always make sure they're disposed of correctly.

With such busy lives and so many things to pay for, convenience and price are usually the main considerations when we go shopping. We're temped by deals and look for the cheapest version of the item we need. Often, though, that cheap item isn't really the most cost-effective option; if it lasts only half the time a higher quality alternative would have, you'll end up repurchasing. It's not always

possible, but invest in longer-lasting goods when you can and you'll help both the planet and your bank account in the long run. A good example of this is the disposable razor – it's marketed as cheap and hygienic, but buy a quality razor and all you'll need to repurchase is the blade.

Fashion

In a recent survey of 18-to-35-year-olds by the Fashion Retail Academy, 71 per cent of participants said they liked the concept of sustainable clothing, but fewer than 40 per cent were actually interested in investing in long-lasting pieces. The fashion industry has an extremely high turnover, with trends constantly changing and pressure put on consumers to keep up. Remarks are made if someone wears the same outfit to multiple events and, while charity shops and thrift shops have seen a recent surge in popularity, brand new is still the default for many shoppers.

If you want to make your wardrobe more sustainable, start by being careful about your shopping choices. Take a moment before purchasing a new item and ask yourself why you're buying it – is it something versatile that will last for years, or are you buying it for a single occasion? Is it a sensible investment, or do you want it because it's on sale and you've had a rubbish day and want to cheer yourself up? Choose timeless, quality garments over bold items that will be out of fashion by the end of the season. Where possible, buy second-hand. When you fall out of love with garments, don't throw them away; donate pieces in good condition to charity and drop worn or damaged ones at a nearby clothes bank for recycling.

Furniture and homeware

'Upcycling' is a fairly new word in our vocabularies and it's become something of a trend, but the principle is an ancient one. Just because something has been slightly damaged or become a little scruffy it doesn't mean it's now useless, and goods don't need to be thrown away as soon as they no longer serve their original purpose. Get creative and find ways to give old goods another lease of life; tired-looking furniture can be repainted or re-covered, holes in clothes can be repaired with bright patches or embroidery, and empty jam jars can become simple and effective vases or tealight holders.

In recent years, a number of 'repair cafés' have sprung up in reaction to the world's increasing waste. These centres of quiet rebellion offer all the tools needed to fix clothes, shoes, furniture and small electrical items. Volunteers with strong repair skills are on hand to offer help and advice, sharing their knowledge so more people have the confidence to try and fix their belongings instead of throwing them away as soon as they become damaged or stop working properly. If there isn't an event near you, there are a multitude of guides and forums online with tips.

Make do & mend

Losing a button doesn't have to signal the end for your favourite garment

- Find the missing button if you can. If not, take the item's spare button or get a matching one.

- Thread a needle with 60cm (24") of thread a similar colour to the button. Pull the thread through until there's an even length on each side, then knot the ends together.

- Position the button on the fabric and hold it in place. Push the needle up through one of the buttonholes from the back of the fabric and pull the thread all the way through.

- Slide a pin between the button and the fabric to stop it being sewn on too tight, then thread the needle down through another hole.

- Add stitches until the button is secure, then push the needle through to the front of the fabric underneath the button – but not through a buttonhole.

- Remove the pin and wrap the thread 5-6 times around the thread between the fabric and the button.

- Make a few small stitches under the button to secure the thread, then cut off the excess.

"Take a moment before purchasing a new item and ask yourself why you're buying it"

Upcycling increases the lifespan of goods and allows for personal touches

£420

THE AMOUNT THE AVERAGE UK HOUSEHOLD THROWS AWAY EACH YEAR BY WASTING FOOD

40 MILLION

THE NUMBER OF UNUSED ELECTRICAL GADGETS THOUGHT TO BE GATHERING DUST IN UK DRAWERS

11,000+

THE NUMBER OF CHARITY SHOPS IN THE UK, FULL OF SECOND-HAND CLOTHES, BOOKS AND HOMEWARE

THE COST OF WASTE

Consumerism drives global economies, but not without consequences

63%

THE PREDICTED RISE IN GLOBAL CONSUMPTION OF NEW CLOTHES BETWEEN NOW AND 2030

£150

THE ESTIMATED AMOUNT A BRITISH WOMAN SPENDS ON DISPOSABLE SANITARY PRODUCTS EACH YEAR

26%

THE PERCENTAGE OF CLOTHES THAT GO UNWORN IN THE AVERAGE BRIT'S WARDROBE

£10-20

THE COST OF A REUSABLE MENSTRUAL CUP, WHICH LASTS FOR AROUND 10 YEARS

OVER 180

THE AVERAGE NUMBER OF PLASTIC ITEMS FOUND ON A 100M STRETCH OF BRITISH BEACH

31KG

THE AMOUNT OF PLASTIC PACKAGING WASTE PRODUCED EACH YEAR BY THE AVERAGE EU RESIDENT

3 BILLION

THE ESTIMATED NUMBER OF DISPOSABLE NAPPIES THROWN AWAY IN THE UK EVERY YEAR

While the rewards of wandering the globe are greater than ever before, so too is the responsibility

Eco-Friendly Travel

As traditional boundaries to travel continue to disappear, and the world grows increasingly interconnected, more people are exploring the planet than ever before. Despite all of the cultural and financial benefits this brings, travel can have devastating consequences, placing some of the world's most delicate landscapes and cultural gems at risk.

Since international travel exploded in 1950, one million species have become threatened, and vulnerable human populations have been driven to the brink of collapse. Thailand's Maya Bay, virtually unknown a few decades ago, in 2018 became so damaged that the government had to close it indefinitely.

In 2016, two-thirds of coral in the northern Great Barrier Reef was declared dead. Peru, meanwhile, has already had to cap visitor numbers at Machu Picchu on account of the substantial damage caused by tourists. One day, it may be closed completely, only viewable from afar.

Travel is a wonderful thing when done right; the greatest mind-expanding experience and ultimate cultural bridge. However, it should serve local communities and ecosystems, not exploit them. Once our natural and cultural treasures are destroyed, it will be too late. The burden to protect them falls on every single traveller, and the time is now.

Sitting at the crossroads of environmental, social and economic issues, eco travel focuses on minimising the impact of tourism. For the uninitiated, it covers all the variants of ecotourism and green travel, including responsible travel, sustainable tourism and ethical travel. While these terms are interchangeable and vary wildly, their principles remain steadfast: minimise your impact, tread lightly and always leave a place better than you found it. It also promotes environmental and cultural awareness, contributing to conservation efforts and the socio-economic development of local communities.

Fortunately, eco travel's star is on the rise. As the public becomes better educated about the impact of travel on the planet, more people are committing to minimising their own footprints. Whether that's staying at a resort that farms its own food, travelling by land rather than by air, or choosing parks where fees are funnelled directly to conservation, there are myriad options for seeking out greener holidays, ensuring future generations can experience the wonders of travel for years to come.

How To Pick A Destination

First, when it comes to choosing a destination, not all are created eco-equal. Some demonstrate a much deeper commitment to Earth-friendly policies, community-centred programmes and sustainable practices than others. Unsurprisingly, Nordic countries lead the pack. Meanwhile, Costa Rica has positioned itself as one of the world's most successful ecotourism destinations. Over 25 per cent of its land – from the beaches of Costa Ballena to rainforests teeming with wildlife – is protected.

Among developing nations, Namibia was the first African country to add the protection of the environment to its constitution, placing conservation at its heart. Meanwhile, 97 per cent of the Galápagos Islands are protected by Ecuador's National Parks Service.

Another emerging eco-Mecca is Uzbekistan. The former Soviet stronghold is now home to a flourishing outdoor culture, with hiking, horseback riding, mountaineering, white-water rafting and bird watching aplenty. It also offers a wealth of alternative accommodation, like eco-friendly yurts, homestays and cooperative-run lodges.

To guide you in selecting the right destination, there are countless rankings listing the world's greenest locales. But, it's just as easy to make an informed decision on your own. Locations with extensive public-transport systems, protected parks, walkable neighbourhoods, and a taste for organic and local produce are usually safe bets. Just avoid the hysterical call to 'go before it's gone'. Travellers flocking to areas that are already endangered – such as the low-lying Pacific Islands threatened by rising tides; the last remaining Wonder of the Ancient World (the Great Pyramid of Giza); and disappearing Arctic glaciers – only contribute to their destruction.

Travel Green

The next challenge is how to get there. There simply aren't any green ways of flying, and CO_2 emissions per passenger are astronomical. While the aviation industry is developing bio-fuelled aircrafts, the best option available is to minimise and offset as much as possible. It also helps to book direct flights where possible, to avoid unnecessary fuel-guzzling take-offs and landings.

Another factor towards shrinking your carbon footprint is which class you fly. First and Business produce nine and three times more carbon emissions than Economy respectively. In addition to forgoing the extra elbowroom in favour of conservationist class, carbon-offset programs can go some way to counteracting flight emissions. These schemes enable individuals to donate to green projects – like solar farms, deforestation taskforces and wind-turbine production – to compensate for their own carbon footprints. Renewable projects are considered best, as they directly address the chief cause of climate change: fossil fuels.

While carbon offsetting is not a long-term solution to the problem, it is an effective way of mitigating damage, if combined with other responsible travel practices. But, with hundreds of offset schemes available, it's important to choose the right one. Airlines like Qantas, Japan Airlines, Delta and Cathay Pacific directly offer customers a way to offset carbon emissions.

Elsewhere, look for projects that are certified Gold Standard, Verified Carbon Standard, Voluntary Gold Standard or Certified Emission Reduction, which means they meet the Kyoto Protocol guidelines, an international treaty committed to reducing greenhouse gas emissions. Schemes, such as Terrapass, Carbon Footprint, Cool Effect and Atmosfair, offer a dynamic range of certified projects to offset against.

Get around your destination

How you travel around once you've landed comes with its own quandaries. Cycling, hiking and walking are greenest, but if you need to travel long distances, trains are generally considered environmentally friendly. Buses carrying upward of 40 passengers are the next-best alternative. The most sustainable systems run on electric or alternative power and boast high passenger rates. Switzerland's hydroelectric-powered trains and hybrid buses, along with Japan's lightweight, high-capacity Shinkansen (bullet train), are among the most notable examples.

For seafarers, cruising the open waters can either be a green dream or an environmental disaster. Though sailboats and catamarans are gentle on the planet, cruise ships empty one billion

"More people are committing to minimising their own carbon footprints"

gallons of sewage into the oceans every year, while leaking petrol into fragile ecosystems. To help combat the damage, Norwegian cruise line Hurtigruten is exploring greener pastures with the construction of three hybrid ships. The first of the three (and the first of its kind), MS Roald Amundsen, made its maiden voyage in 2019.

Where To Stay

Finding a hotel with an environmental conscience is easy enough, but trusting them with your eco-conscious pennies is more difficult, thanks to less-than-honest proprietors greenwashing their supposed Earth-friendly practices. One way to check out your accommodation's green credentials is through certification programmes. While the Green Hotels Association issues LEED (Leadership in Energy and Environmental Design) certifications to hotels that put environment conservation into practice, Green Key and the Global Sustainable Tourism Council also verify lodgings truly deserving of their eco-warrior status.

Choosing green accommodation doesn't necessarily mean forgoing a hot shower or other mod cons. Instead, travellers should focus on the issues that matter the most to them, and select accommodation that matches those priorities. While eco-lodges and homestays are often the most sustainable options, many hotel chains and independent properties offer green programmes, such as in-room recycling, composting or only sourcing local produce. Small luxury groups, like Aman, Six Senses and Alila, follow rigorous green practices, while mainstream chains like Accor, Rosewood and IHG have implemented sustainability strategies.

Making environmentally friendly decisions throughout a stay is just as important as choosing the right transport and accommodation. If doing laundry is a must, take clothes to a local facility that supports job creation, and ditch disposable water bottles in favour of BPA-free filtration systems, like Grayl, Lifesaver and LifeStraw.

What To Do

When it comes to sightseeing, there are always plenty of options that are gentle on Mother Nature, like snorkelling, scuba diving, hiking, swimming, kayaking, biking and bird-watching. In addition, visiting craft fairs or markets and purchasing locally produced, artisanal goods supports indigenous communities and farmers – just don't forget to take a reusable bag. When hunger calls, dine at eco-conscious, fair-labour eateries that serve up locally sourced ingredients.

Finally, when hiring tour companies, avoid international operators and opt for local, environmentally friendly businesses that employ, and fairly compensate, local guides. Not only are you empowering the native population and helping to generate income, but you'll learn from a guide with a deep-rooted knowledge and understanding of the destination, and so you will receive a far more authentic experience.

How to be...
A Globetrotting Vegan

Though the world is waking up to veganism, some places are definitely easier for veggies and vegans to enjoy than others...

In New Zealand, Tauranga attracts plenty of surfers and hippies to its stunning shores

1 Tauranga, New Zealand

The Antipodean nation of New Zealand is known across the world for its beautiful scenery, friendly people, and liberal outlook. Tauranga, a small city on the Bay of Plenty, is a gorgeous place surrounded by the blue waters of the South Pacific. Not only that, it's great for vegans – you'll find plenty of plant-based restaurants, coffee shops and takeaways in the Harbourside part of town. Enjoy a vegan wrap as the sun sets over the water, or a healthy smoothie in the shade of Mount Maunganui.

2 Delhi, India

India has a long history of vegetarianism. Many of its religions – including Hinduism and Jainism – advocate a vegetarian diet. Within that, there are plenty of vegan options available (such as lentil daal, chana masala and vegetable biryani), and these should be clearly marked on menus. If not, don't be afraid to ask the restaurant staff, who will be understanding of your dietary needs.

If you're looking for a quick fix, look no further than India's incredible street food, or even have your lunch delivered in a tiffin as busy Delhi workers do. While North Indian food has some incredible veggie options, South Indian food is arguably even better for vegans, so be sure to try that too.

Delhi's Red Fort is one of the most beautiful Mughal attractions in the city

Best of the rest

Athens, Greece

Though Greece wasn't really known for vegan food, the last five years have seen Athens transform into a vegan-friendly destination. Head over to Lime Bistro in Thiseio to enjoy vegan takes on traditional dishes.

Amman, Jordan

There's so much more to Jordan than the classic hummus, but it's a very good place to start. Many restaurants nowadays offer vegan options, such as grilled aubergine, and even delicious vegan burgers.

Montreal's old town is as charming as it is picturesque

As Brazil's financial centre, São Paulo is home to many swish skyscrapers

Montreal, Canada

Brush up on your French, you're going to Montreal. The Québécois city is one of the most culturally rich cities in all Canada, but its youthful vibe will keep you enthralled. In Montreal, food from around the world meets in the lovely city centre – you can try Vietnamese Pho, vegan falafel pittas, and dairy-free creamy Italian pasta within walking distance of each other. But the first thing you must eat on any trip to Canada is a veganised replication of the national dish, Poutine – which is French Fries, cheese curds, and gravy. Sounds like a weird combination, but trust us – you won't be able to get enough of Montreal's legendary vegan versions.

São Paulo, Brazil

Brazil's super-modern financial hub definitely keeps up to date with food trends. In such a cosmopolitan city, inhabited by people from as far away as Italy, Japan, and the Arab world, you're bound to find something that tickles your tastebuds. Savour a plate of warm, classically Brazilian black bean stew, with wholesome brown rice and vegetables. Or, if you'd like to try some of São Paulo's legendary vegan fusion food, you must head to Sushimar Vegano to try Japanese-Brazilian sushi.

Ubud, Indonesia

Bali is visited by millions of international tourists every year, for its beaches, jungles, and incredible history. This international flavour means it's great for vegans, but many of Bali's Buddhist and Hindu locals also practise vegetarianism. So, once you've finished exploring an ancient temple, or doing a relaxing yoga class, you'll find plenty of options for your dinner. Besides raw burgers, piping hot tofu stir fries and spicy curries, you'll find sumptuous vegan ice creams and cheesecakes to have for afters. If you're there in October, be sure to attend the annual Bali Vegan Festival, where you can share some gorgeous street food with other vegan travellers.

Bali's religious landmarks will take your breath away

Berlin, Germany

You won't struggle to find vegan food in Berlin. More or less every eatery will have at least one vegan option, and there's no shortage of purely vegan cafes and restaurants, either.

Singapore, Singapore

Singapore's melting pot of cultures – Tamil, Malay and Chinese – means its food is as diverse as its people. There's vegetarian South Indian fare everywhere, and you must try the Loving Hut for a completely vegan Chinese experience.

Kingston, Jamaica

Many Rastafarians believe humans are natural vegetarians, and some follow a vegan diet. You'll find plenty of healthy and delicious options here – check out the plantain and vegetable stews on offer.